THE PLAIN PEOPLE
OF THE CONFEDERACY

SOUTHERN CLASSICS SERIES
John G. Sproat, General Editor

THE

PLAIN PEOPLE

OF THE

CONFEDERACY

Bell Irvin Wiley

with a new introduction by Paul Escott

UNIVERSITY OF SOUTH CAROLINA PRESS
*Published in cooperation with the Institute for
Southern Studies and the South Caroliniana Society
of the University of South Carolina.*

© 1943 Louisiana State University Press, Baton Rouge
© 1963 Quadrangle Books, Inc., Chicago
© 1971 Peter Smith, Gloucester, Massachusetts
© 2000 John F. Wiley

Introduction © 2000 University of South Carolina

Published in Columbia, South Carolina, by the
University of South Carolina Press in cooperation with the
Institute for Southern Studies and the South Caroliniana
Society of the University of South Carolina

Manufactured in the United States of America

04 03 02 01 00   5 4 3 2 1

LIBRARY OF CONGRESS CATALOGING-IN-PUBLICATION DATA

Wiley, Bell Irvin, 1906–
    The plain people of the Confederacy / Bell Irvin Wiley;
with a new introduction by Paul Escott.
        p.   cm. — (Southern classics series)
    Originally published: Baton Rouge: Louisiana State
University, 1943.
    Includes bibliographical references and index.
    ISBN 1-57003-362-5 (alk. paper)
    1. Confederate States of America—Social conditions.
2. United States—History—Civil War, 1861–1865—Social
aspects.   3. Soldiers—Confederate States of America—
Social conditions.   4. Afro-Americans—Confederate States
of America—Social conditions.   5. Women—Confederate
States of America—Social conditions.   I. Title.   II. Series.
F214 .W56   2000
973.7' 13—dc21   00-028622

To
Big George and Miss Amy

CONTENTS

[vii]

SERIES EDITOR'S PREFACE

Bell Wiley's *Plain People of the Confederacy* affirms the adage that "good things come in small packages." Interpretive and provocative, yet grounded in impeccable scholarship, this brief examination of the Confederate home front is a pioneering consideration of the conflict between myth and reality that has always shadowed southern perceptions of the Civil War. In Paul Escott's splendid introduction to this edition, readers will find an incisive and fair-minded assessment of Wiley's judgments, as well as ample evidence that the book deserves recognition as a Southern Classic.

* * *

Southern Classics returns to general circulation books of importance dealing with the history and culture of the American South. Sponsored by the Institute for Southern Studies and the South Caroliniana Society of the University of South Carolina, the series is advised by a board of distinguished scholars, whose members suggest titles and editors of individual volumes to the

General Editor and help to establish priorities in publication.

Chronological age alone does not determine a title's designation as a Southern Classic. The criteria include, as well, significance in contributing to a broad understanding of the region, timeliness in relation to events and moments of peculiar interest to the American South, usefulness in the classroom, and suitability for inclusion in personal and institutional collections on the region.

JOHN G. SPROAT
General Editor, *Southern Classics Series*

INTRODUCTION

Few events in American history have produced as many myths as the Civil War. The war seared the nation's soul, engaging powerful and long-lasting emotions. Although the costs of the conflict were enormous in human as well as material terms, the suffering of a single generation cannot explain its enduring power over American thought. The significance of the war lies even deeper—entangled with the generations that came before and after the 1860s. Fundamental conflicts and issues that continue to challenge American society were irrevocably tied to the war. Its results added new layers of controversy to old divisions. More than with most events, the Civil War was not simply history or something in the past. It continued to matter and thus spawned new argument, advocacy, and myth.

In 1961, as the centennial of this great conflict approached, one of the South's leading literary figures reflected on its legacy in the American imagination. Robert Penn Warren argued that the Civil War was "an overwhelming and vital image" and "our only 'felt' history—history lived in the national imagination." Yet he was quick to point out that it had not been felt in the same way by different groups of Americans. Summarizing decades of political and cultural controversy in two useful phrases, Warren identified the contrasting interpretations of the war that North and South have found useful. "To give things labels," Warren wrote, "we may say that the War gave the South the Great Alibi and gave the North the Treasury of Virtue."[1]

For the North, victorious in a conflict that saved the Union and brought about the emancipation of almost four million slaves, the war was lasting proof of good character. Looking back on the era with a self-interested gaze and present-oriented perspective, northerners could cite the war to counter any criticism of their shortcomings. Ignoring the complexities of history, they could depict the conflict as "a consciously undertaken crusade so full of righteousness that there is enough overplus stored to Heaven . . . to take care of all small failings and oversights . . . unto the present generation." The Treasury of Virtue allowed northerners to feel "automatically redeemed . . . for all sins past, present, and future."[2]

Seductive as the Treasury of Virtue may have been for northerners, the Great Alibi had even greater usefulness for southerners. Defeated in battle, stigmatized as rebels or traitors, and buffeted by shifting economic currents after the war, southerners faced painful criticism on many sides. It became tempting to find an excuse for the region's problems that was rooted in an event of undeniable magnitude. It became useful to explain away unpleasant realities by attributing them to the destruction and lasting impact of the war. By use of the Great Alibi, Warren wrote, the "common lyncher becomes a defender of the Southern tradition," and "pellagra, hookworm, and illiteracy are all explained, or explained away, and mortgages are converted into badges of distinction."[3]

Robert Penn Warren focused mainly on the Civil War's capacity to spawn myths that interpreted subsequent history or put a gloss on events occurring long after 1865. But the war generated myths even as it was taking place. Or, to be more accurate, from an early date people created mythical views of the war to interpret their motives, justify their conduct, or bolster their morale. Southerners especially manifested a need to propound explanations or interpretations for secession, war, and defeat. Robert Penn Warren could well have argued that mythmaking encompassed the South's experience during the war and shaped people's memories of the nature of the Confederacy.

To cite only a few examples, southerners were very concerned to explain the causes of secession in high-minded and defensible terms. Although the papers of southern leaders reveal that anxiety over the protection of slavery was their primary motive for secession, most public figures stressed constitutional principles. Jefferson Davis took the lead in arguing that the Confederacy had come into being to protect constitutional liberty. With defeat, this position became even more important. In 1866 the Virginia novelist John Esten Cooke took care to defend "the right of secession" in his novel *Surry of Eagle's-Nest.* Almost forty years later another Virginia writer, Thomas Nelson Page, acknowledged that "[i]t is important to make clear that the right did exist, because on this depends the South's place in history. Without this we were mere insurgents and rebels; with it, we were a great people in revolution for our rights."[4]

Likewise, those who fought the war for the South were noble figures—gallant, brave, and chivalrous; white southerners wanted to establish that in no way were they traitorous. This was a central theme of the defeated soldiers who organized the postwar Southern

Historical Society.[5] Going further, a variety of writers developed and enlarged the image of J. E. B. Stuart as a medieval knight in modern times. To a succession of southern authors, Stuart was more than a bold and daring cavalry commander—he was a veritable knight of chivalry who stepped forth from the pages of medieval romance. Stuart's dash and penchant for romanticizing himself in this manner certainly contributed to his image, but the image of a "cavalier *par excellence*," a "knight 'without reproach or fear'" also bolstered a helpful myth. While others looked down on them as defeated rebels, white southerners could celebrate the "courtesy" and "indifference to danger" of one of their heroes who "like some chevalier of olden days, rode to battle with his lady's glove upon his helm, humming a song, and determined to conquer or fall."[6]

The nature of slavery was a crucial subject for myth, and southern writers used their craft to counter the abolitionists' descriptions of the cruelty of slavery. George Cary Eggleston, in essays in the *Atlantic Monthly*, described the prewar plantation as the site of "a soft, dreamy, deliciously quiet life . . . with all its sharp corners and rough surfaces long ago worn round and smooth." According to Thomas Nelson Page, life on the plantation had a "singular sweetness and freedom from vice." It was "replete with happiness and content. . . . Its graces were never equalled." And, of course, Page created in 1881 the character of Sam, the contented, happy slave who kept alive the memory of his beloved Marse Chan and remained devoted in freedom to his white family. Referring to his time in slavery, Sam testified that "'[d]em wuz good ole times, marster—de bes' Sam ever see! . . . Dyar warn' no trouble nor nothin.'"[7]

In accord with these myths, there grew up an image or set of assumptions about the Confederacy that became part of the popular understanding of the Civil War. Because principled and chivalrous southerners seceded in devotion to principle, it was assumed that there was unity within the Confederacy. The people of the South fought bravely and effectively until they were overwhelmed "by numbers." The Confederacy's soldiers were loyal, brave, and dedicated, and its citizens readily sacrificed for the cause. Due to the "relation of warm friendship and tender sympathy" that existed between master and slave, the black people of the Confederacy protected their white folks and remained overwhelmingly loyal during the war—by a ratio of at least one hundred to one.[8]

These myths were powerful. Given the strong emotions that survived the war and the emotional need of
white southerners to regain their standing as respected
equals in the Union, such images took a deep hold on
the region. Repeated widely in literature and even
more frequently in family and neighborhood conver-
sations, they became background "facts"—ideas that
were accepted as true without question. Even more,
their acceptance was equated with respectability and
loyalty to the region; only the hostile northerner or
unfriendly troublemaker would question the South's
role in the war or the glorious legacy that was embod-
ied in the Confederate experience.

By anyone's assessment Bell Irvin Wiley was a
southerner through and through. Born in Halls, Tennessee, in 1906, he grew up in a society keenly attuned
to the mythology and controversy surrounding the
South's history. Undoubtedly he took in many of the
region's orthodox beliefs about the Confederacy along
with the air that he breathed. As a young man he
earned his undergraduate degree at Asbury College, in
Wilmore, Kentucky, a liberal arts college founded in
the Wesleyan-Arminian and Holiness traditions and
imbued with orthodox evangelical Christian principles. Graduating in 1928, Wiley went to the University

of Kentucky to earn a master's degree and then received his Ph.D. from Yale in 1933. Throughout his distinguished career as a historian he held permanent appointments exclusively at southern institutions. Beginning in 1934 at Mississippi Southern College, Wiley moved on to the University of Mississippi in 1938 and then to Louisiana State University in 1946. In 1949 he began twenty-five years of service at Emory University and after his retirement taught at Agnes Scott College. Long active in and honored by the Southern Historical Association, Bell Wiley was a southerner as well as a historian of the South.[9]

His background did not prevent him, however, from taking a fresh and searching look at the Confederate experience, and this is one of the reasons *The Plain People of the Confederacy* remains a significant and engaging book. With impressive richness of detail, Wiley painted a picture of the Confederacy that differed sharply from the myth. Not only did he document aspects of military history and the soldiers' story that were inconsistent with the orthodox southern version of events, but he also presented the home front in new and startling ways. The Confederacy that Bell Wiley, historian, revealed was a far more complex, conflicted, and intriguing society than the version that prevailed in the regional consciousness. It also was a picture of the Confederacy that must have shocked and angered many prosouthern patriots. Those who were more interested in fighting battles for regional prestige than in examining the historical record must have detested this influential little book.

In radically revising deeply held southern myths, Bell Wiley deserves credit for being a pioneer. Though not the first, his book was one of the early studies that opened new vistas for our understanding of the Confederacy. Ella Lonn's and Bessie Martin's studies of desertion had been published in 1928 and 1932, respectively. Careful examinations of political conflict in the Confederacy, such as Frank Owsley's *State Rights in the Confederacy* and Albert Burton Moore's *Conscription and Conflict in the Confederacy* had appeared in the mid-1920s. In 1937 Charles H. Wesley's *The Collapse of the Confederacy* was published. But Wiley's *The Plain People of the Confederacy,* published in 1944, focused more exclusively and broadly on social history than these other important works. Based on the Walter Lynwood Fleming Lectures given by Wiley at Louisiana State University, it appeared in print at almost the same time as Charles Ramsdell's *Behind the Lines in the Southern Confederacy.* Thus, in a meaningful way, Wiley's work was a pioneering study offering a fresh interpretation.[10]

In 1943 Wiley had published *The Life of Johnny Reb: The Common Soldier of the Confederacy*, a classic that revealed his penchant for realism, fact, and a balanced assessment based on deep knowledge of historical sources.[11] He began *The Plain People of the Confederacy* with a respectful chapter on the common soldier. In it he recited the many factors that made soldiers' lives difficult. Food was scarce and often of poor quality; supplies of clothing or shoes soon became inadequate; vermin and insects caused constant irritation; and disease was a greater threat than bullets. Moreover, "the incompetency and highhandedness of officers" made soldiering intolerable for some and dangerous for others. Even when they were not in danger, privates struggled with the boredom of camp life. Confederate soldiers did not have an easy time, but "taken as a whole the fighting record of the men who wore the gray was a good one."[12]

Wiley made clear, however, that the record was not identical to the myth. Despite the bravery of many, there was the normal amount of human cowardice within Confederate ranks, and the vices that have characterized military encampments through human history were part of the southern army. While on the march southern troops plundered the farms of their countrymen and the homes of Yankees, despite Lee's orders. Moreover, many soldiers were not dedicated and loyal, for "morale sank to a very low ebb during the latter half of the war. The initial wave of patriotism that swept over the Confederacy after Fort Sumter was not of long duration. War-weariness began to creep into home letters after a few months, and . . . [t]he Conscription Act of April, 1862, . . . was a severe blow to morale. . . . [T]he reverses of Gettysburg and Vicksburg the following year brought unprecedented gloom."[13] As the war dragged on, "leave-taking" increased. Deserters numbered over one hundred thousand, and many of these became outliers who "flaunted Confederate authority for the duration of the war."[14] This gap between myth and reality was prominent in Wiley's treatment of black southerners and the home front as well.

As social history *The Plain People of the Confederacy* retains some freshness even today. Its perspective on race must have been zestful—and downright shocking to many—in 1944. Wiley took seriously the humanity and dignity of African Americans and documented their strivings for freedom and autonomy in the Confederacy. In the process he exploded some of the treasured shibboleths of southern writers and regional patriots. After recounting the tendency of slaves to flee to federal lines and describing the deterioration of plantation discipline during the war, Wiley explicitly challenged the myth of the loyal and contented slave. "Most of the slaves earnestly desired freedom," he wrote, "and when it came within safe and convenient reach they seized upon it with alacrity." Instances of slaves who hid the family silver and protected the white women and children "were exceptional, and restricted largely to the house servants who, because of their privileged status, had perhaps more to lose than to win by freedom." "All in all," Wiley declared, "the reaction of slaves to the coming of the Federals was such as to reveal to the whites how little they knew of the real feelings so effectively concealed behind the veil of smiles and obsequious manners. . . . Before the war was over most whites living in areas penetrated by Federal troops had abundant reason to feel as did an Alabaman who in 1863 complained that 'the "faithful slave" is about played out.'"[15]

Despite outmoded vocabulary that is avoided today, Wiley's treatment of enslaved southerners shows that he had broken with the racial stereotypes that dominated white southern thought in the era of segregation. His research for *Southern Negroes, 1861–1865* (published in 1938) had been extensive and penetrating. As a result his summary in *The Plain People of the Confederacy* of the major events in the experience of black southerners during the war clearly identified all major elements in their struggle for freedom. Even fine points in the military experience of black people received accurate attention. For example, Wiley noted that the Confederate law authorizing the recruitment of black soldiers was "silent on the subject of emancipation."[16] For the federal army he noted the varieties of discrimination that African Americans experienced even as they were risking their lives for the preservation of the Union. A few of Wiley's comments and choices of words offend our sensibilities at the end of the twentieth century, but he deserves to be judged in comparison to the standards of his day, not ours.[17] By that standard his treatment of black southerners was very progressive.

Similarly, it is notable that Wiley considered the women of the Confederacy an important topic for historical analysis. He did not, of course, write what would today be called women's history or produce a gendered interpretation, but he acted upon the conviction that the experience of southern women in the war was important. Taking their lives and problems seriously, he documented their suffering and showed how vitally it affected the entire Confederate cause. From his research Wiley understood that the war drastically affected the conditions of everyday life for the Confederacy's "plain people." At the outset of his chapter "The Folk at Home," Wiley detailed changes in diet that began as inconveniences but soon amounted to serious "scarcity of food." He understood the "deprivation and hunger suffered by the wives and mothers of the poorest soldiers" and documented both the extent and the failure of efforts at poor relief. Moreover, he recognized that plummeting morale was a notable problem "particularly among the wives and mothers of soldiers." So serious was this problem on the home front that it affected the armies in the field. In these ways Wiley came close to anticipating recent interpretations that place the outlook of women at the center of the Confederacy's failure.[18]

Even today some Civil War historians assume that "the paucity of testimony from the yeomanry and from poorer Confederates frustrates efforts to speak confidently about them."[19] Bell Wiley knew that was not the case. In his research he had unearthed a wealth of data on the yeomanry and ordinary citizens. His short chapter on the home front described wartime changes in dress, schooling, amusements, courtship, religious life, and public morality. Moreover, he quoted liberally from materials in which the plain people directly and forcefully gave their testimony. Drawing on letters to North Carolina's governor Zebulon Vance, Wiley illustrated the rich sources that exist in government files as well as in private correspondence, newspapers, and other documents. Historians can, indeed, obtain the testimony of ordinary Confederate citizens, and that testimony tells a story that continues to be relevant to vital issues about the Confederacy.[20]

Wiley brought to center stage the issue of popular morale. He insisted on its importance in shaping the fate of the Confederacy, and he offered a strong interpretation of the reasons for discontent. Contrary to the myth of a unified South with a determined and self-sacrificing citizenry, Wiley showed that the Confederacy had been racked with dissension and that the deterioration of support for the war reached truly alarming proportions. Moreover, the heart of the problem lay in class resentments, even more than military reverses.

At the beginning of the war, such had not been the case. The poor folk of the Confederacy "supported the war in its early stages with no less zeal than their upper-class neighbors." But after the first year, Wiley asserted, "there was a notable defection of spirit, particularly among the wives and mothers of soldiers." No one who has read extensively in sources about the home front can deny the accuracy of Wiley's assertion. Similarly, few would question his conclusion that "by the summer of 1864, if not sooner, the majority of them would probably have welcomed peace on the basis of emancipation of slaves and the restoration of the Union."[21]

What caused such serious disaffection? Wiley argued for several factors, but "paramount" among them was "the feeling that privileged groups, particularly the planters, were shirking their military responsibilities." He pointed to the ill-advised law that gave an exemption from military service to the owners of twenty slaves as the primary cause of a sense of injustice. Other factors deepened the discontent, as for example, "the failure of planters to meet the requisitions of army leaders for Negroes to work on fortifications." As daily life for the plain people became a struggle to survive, the privileges of the rich became more galling. Thousands shared the feelings of a farmer who asked Governor Vance for a furlough to harvest his small crop. "How can we go in to battle," this soldier asked, when the "rich man" who "owns twenty negros is permitted to stay at home with his family and save his grain but the [poor] man must suffer in the armmy for somthing to eat [with] his family suffering at home for somthing to eat."²²

Another factor that played a major role was alarm over speculation and extortion—"the conviction that the 'big folk' were using the war to enhance their riches."²³ The hoarding of foodstuffs while thousands went hungry aroused bitter anger. Despair over the suffering of loved ones in the army also depressed morale. Likewise, military defeats obviously played a role. Wiley did not neglect the contribution of military defeats to declining morale; rather, he traced a downward trajectory of the people's hopes that was linked to the battlefield. The defeats at Gettysburg and Vicksburg "were depressing enough," he wrote, but morale plummeted after the fall of Atlanta. The hardships that weighed relentlessly on the poorer women of the Confederacy were "a final and significant factor," he argued.²⁴

Wiley's last paragraph in "The Folk at Home" showed how seriously he viewed these issues: "Two of the greatest mistakes of the Confederate government were the refusal to exempt from conscription non-slaveholding adult males upon whose labor the livelihood of wives and small children was vitally dependent, and the failure to take effective measures against hoarding and speculation. Dissatisfaction arising from these sins of omission did more than anything else to break down the morale of the civilian masses. Long before the finale at Appomattox, the doom of the Confederacy had been firmly sealed by the widespread defection of her humblest subjects."[25]

How well has Wiley's interpretation on these critical matters stood the test of time? Historians naturally reassess and reevaluate the past, and a number of recent works challenge the broadness of some of Wiley's wording. In his recent publications James McPherson has criticized sweeping, deterministic arguments and insisted on the importance of contingency in shaping the outcome of the Civil War. The "dimension of *contingency*," he argues, requires "the recognition that at numerous critical points during the war things might have gone altogether differently." McPherson identifies times at which events on the battlefield or political and diplomatic developments threatened to turn the tide. In particular he asks readers to remember how close the North came in 1864 "to the brink of peace negotiations and the election of a Democratic president."[26] Acknowledging that the Confederacy was weakened by internal dissensions, McPherson insists on reminding us that the North was struggling with its problems as well.

On his point about contingency, McPherson is surely right. Both North and South faced formidable problems and disappointing reverses, and the outcome of the Civil War remained in question until very late in the contest. As the war dragged on and its costs mounted, the determination and resources of both sections were tested. Like two weary fighters staggering through the last rounds of a prizefight, the Union and Confederate governments had a difficult time marshaling their determination and carrying on to the end. Although statistics on economic and physical resources give the North an enormous advantage, the benefits of those assets were surprisingly difficult to discern through most of the war. Perhaps it is impossible to say that any factor "firmly sealed" the Confederacy's doom or assured the Union's victory.

What, then, was the significance of the class resentments and internal dissension that Wiley described? Identifying internal divisions with "loss of will," James McPherson has argued against the "loss of will thesis" as an adequate explanation of the Confederacy's defeat. It suffers, he contends, from the "fallacy of reversability—that of putting the horse before the cart. Defeat causes demoralization and loss of will; victory pumps up morale and the will to win." Gary Gallagher also has questioned the extent of demoralization in the South, advancing the idea that a strong Confederate identity came to be centered in Robert E. Lee's army.[27] At first glance it appears that Bell Wiley's interpretations do not enjoy the favor of contemporary scholars.

Such a conclusion would be hasty, however, and would give insufficient weight to the broadly based research that he summarized in *The Plain People of the Confederacy*. In some respects Bell Wiley and James McPherson are not very far apart. McPherson wrote that "the capture of Atlanta and Sheridan's destruction of Early's army in the Shenandoah Valley clinched matters for the North. Only then did it become possible to speak of the inevitability of Union victory. Only then did the South experience an irretrievable 'loss of the will to fight.'"[28] Similarly, Bell Wiley noted that several southern defeats had a depressing impact on morale, "but," he writes, "the fall of Atlanta and Hood's defeat in Tennessee utterly destroyed the hope of many people."[29] Thus, they both assign an important role to the results of battle, and they agree on the point at which southern morale was irretrievably damaged.

What is notable about Wiley's argument is that he insists that internal divisions based on class resentments *preceded* the demoralization of military losses and were fundamentally more important. The first of these assertions is testable against the body of evidence, and few careful students of Confederate society would question Wiley's conclusion. If many southerners came to identify Lee's army with southern nationality, there were many more who loudly registered their protests about inequities and privilege even before Lee became a hero. The rise of broadly based, serious disaffection not only preceded the Confederacy's most serious disasters but also took place before most of the South's significant military triumphs. A large body of scholarship supports Bell Wiley on this significant issue of timing.[30]

To assess the importance of internal divisions to the Confederacy's ultimate demise is to form a judgment embracing many complex matters. We can expect the argument about such judgments to continue indefinitely, for that is the nature of historians and the stuff of history. But there is no doubt that Bell Wiley's slim but cogent book played a major role in putting the argument permanently into play and inspiring further research. Evidence for the scope and extent of internal division continues to appear, as for example, in Kenneth C. Martis's atlas of the Confederate Congresses. This volume uses color-coded maps to depict with striking clarity the decline of support for Confederate measures, on issue after issue, in every area that the government controlled.[31]

The Plain People of the Confederacy will continue to impress readers today, and well it should. The thesis that Bell Wiley argues was neither controversial nor surprising to the southerners about whom he wrote. To many of them its truth was all too painfully obvious. Experiencing the bitter divisions Wiley described, those in the government struggled against the demoralization he documented. Among the most intelligent and sober Confederate officials was John A. Campbell, former justice of the United States Supreme Court and assistant secretary of war for the nascent southern nation. In September 1863 he received from his subordinates another in a series of reports on the rise of disaffection and resistance to Confederate authority. Before forwarding this document to Pres. Jefferson Davis, Campbell added a terse and carefully considered endorsement: "The condition of things in the mountain districts of North Carolina, South Carolina, Georgia, and Alabama menaces the existence of The Confederacy as fatally as either of the armies of the United States. This report does not state the danger as so imminent as it has been stated in a number of letters that have been received at this Department."[32] Campbell's testimony is sufficient evidence of the gravity and importance of the social forces that Bell Wiley analyzed more than fifty-five years ago. We remain in his debt for the clarity, brevity, and analytical power of *The Plain People of the Confederacy.*

NOTES

1. Robert Penn Warren, *The Legacy of the Civil War: Meditations on the Centennial* (New York: Random House, 1961), pp. 4, 54.

2. Ibid., pp. 64, 59.

3. Ibid., p. 54.

4. See Paul D. Escott, *After Secession: Jefferson Davis and the Failure of Confederate Nationalism* (Baton Rouge: Louisiana State University Press, 1978), pp. 6, 12, 34–41; John Esten Cooke, *Surry of Eagle's-Nest* (New York: G.W. Dillingham, 1894 [1866]), pp. 13, 117–18, 457–58; Thomas Nelson Page, *The Negro: The Southerner's Problem* (New York: Charles Scribner's Sons, 1904), pp. 207–8.

5. Thomas L. Connelly, *The Marble Man: Robert E. Lee and His Image in American Society* (New York: Knopf, 1977), pp. 72–91 passim.

6. See Escott, "The Uses of Gallantry: Virginians and the Origins of J. E. B. Stuart's Historical Image," *Virginia Magazine of History and Biography,* vol. 103, no. 1 (January 1995), pp. 47–72; quotations from pp. 58 and 59.

7. George Cary Eggleston, *A Rebel's Recollections* (Bloomington: Indiana University Press, 1959 [1878]), pp. 27–28; Page, *The Old South* (New York: Charles Scribner's Sons, 1892, 1919), pp. 167, 184; Page, "Marse Chan" from *In Ole Virginia* (New York: Charles Scribner's Sons, 1887, 1916), p. 10. On the dating of "Marse Chan," see Michael Flusche, "Thomas Nelson Page: The Quandary of a Literary Gentleman," *Virginia Magazine of History and Biography,* vol. 84 (1976), p. 470.

8. See Cooke, *Surry of Eagle's-Nest,* p. 326; Gaines Foster, *Ghosts of the Confederacy: Defeat, the Lost Cause, and the Emergence of the New South, 1865–1913* (New York and Oxford: Oxford University Press, 1987), p. 57; Connelly, *The Marble Man,* p. 91; Page, *The Negro,* pp. 166, 186.

9. Asbury College, "The Statement of Faith" and "The Asbury Heritage," online at http://www.asbury.edu/admin/regist/bulletin/faith.htm and http://www.asbury.edu/admin/regist/bulletin/heritage.htm, September 8, 1999; Jacques Cattell Press, ed., *Directory of American Scholars,* seventh edition (New York and London: R.R. Bowker, 1978), vol. 1, p. 738.

10. Ella Lonn, *Desertion During the Civil War* (New York: Century, 1928); Bessie Martin, *Desertion of Alabama Troops from the Confederate Army: A Study in Sectionalism* (New York: Columbia University Press, 1932); Frank Lawrence Owsley, *State Rights in the Confederacy* (Chicago: University of Chicago Press, 1925); Albert Burton Moore, *Conscription and Conflict in the Confederacy* (New York: Macmillan, 1925); Charles W. Ramsdell, *Behind the Lines in the Southern Confederacy,* edited by Wendell H. Stephenson (Baton Rouge: Louisiana State University Press, 1944).

11. Bell Irvin Wiley, *The Life of Johnny Reb: The Common Soldier of the Confederacy* (Indianapolis: Bobbs-Merrill, 1943).

12. Wiley, *The Plain People of the Confederacy* (Baton Rouge: Louisiana State University Press, 1944), pp. 4–16, 12, 34.

13. Ibid., pp. 22–23, 24–26, 29–30.

14. Ibid., pp. 29–31.

15. Ibid., pp. 83, 84, 85.

16. Ibid., p. 102. For an exploration of all aspects of this issue, see Robert F. Durden, *The Gray and the Black* (Baton Rouge: Louisiana State University Press, 1972).

17. An example of the offensive is his statement that "[t]he numerous slaves of R. F. W. Allston of South Carolina seem to have reverted to a state of savagery when the Federals arrived." Wiley, *The Plain People of the Confederacy*, p. 80.

18. Ibid., pp. 39, 42, 43–44, 64. Drew Faust has argued that southern white "women would not assent indefinitely to the increasing sacrifice and self-denial the Civil War came to require.... It may well have been because of its women that the South lost the Civil War." See Drew Gilpin Faust, "Altars of Sacrifice: Confederate Women and the Narratives of War," *Journal of American History* 76:4 (March 1990), pp. 1200–1228, quotation from page 1228.

19. This quotation is from Gary W. Gallagher, *The Confederate War* (Cambridge and London: Harvard University Press, 1997), p. 72. Gallagher's book, though filled with interesting material and ideas, is limited by what is primarily a military historian's approach to sources, and those soldiers who stayed in the ranks were, as Gallagher points out, among the most committed of Confederates.

20. Wiley, *The Plain People of the Confederacy*, pp. 44 ff. Another particularly rich and interesting source of information on ordinary southern citizens is the collection entitled "Letters Received, Confederate Secretary of War" in the National Archives. This author surveyed only a fraction of

the material in this large collection when researching *After Secession.*

21. Wiley, *The Plain People of the Confederacy,* p. 64.

22. Ibid., p. 65.

23. Ibid., p. 65.

24. Ibid., pp. 66–67.

25. Ibid., p. 69.

26. James M. McPherson, *Battle Cry of Freedom* (New York: Oxford University Press, 1988), p. 858.

27. Ibid.; Gallagher, *The Confederate War,* pp. 72–75, 85–95, 110–11.

28. McPherson, *Battle Cry of Freedom,* p. 858.

29. Wiley, *The Plain People of the Confederacy,* p. 67.

30. I present much of this evidence in *After Secession: Jefferson Davis and the Failure of Confederate Nationalism* (Baton Rouge: Louisiana State University Press, 1978).

31. Kenneth C. Martis, *The Historical Atlas of the Congresses of the Confederate States of America: 1861–1865* (New York: Simon & Schuster, 1994).

32. *The War of the Rebellion: A Compilation of the Official Records of the Union and Confederate Armies,* 130 vols. (Washington: Government Printing Office, 1880–1901), series 4, vol. 2, p. 786.

PREFACE

The common folk, white and black, constituted the bone and sinew of the Southern Confederacy. White yeomen comprised the bulk of the armies that followed Lee in Virginia, Joe Johnston in the central South, and Kirby Smith beyond the Mississippi. These rustics were not all exemplary soldiers by any means. Some of them were overly fond of liquor; others were impervious to discipline; thousands absented themselves without leave; many preferred filth to cleanliness; hundreds played the coward when the bullets whistled close. But on the whole they were good fighters. It is not too much to say that the record of the Confederacy on the field of battle must stand or fall on the basis of their performance.

The wives, children, parents, and other home connections of the plain soldiers composed the overwhelming majority of the South's civilian population. These people had many rough edges. Many could not write. Their speech was usually crude and their manners unpolished. But they had many virtues. For the most part they were sturdy, hardworking, respectable citizens. During the early years of the war they were staunch in their support of the Southern cause. After Gettysburg and Vicksburg their patriotism dwindled. But their defection probably was due more to the conviction that they were being discriminated against by the privileged classes than to defeats or deprivations.

The colored folk constituted about a third of the Confederacy's populace. They were not the docile, "Old Kentucky Home" type of subservients that romancers have depicted them to be. Most of them idealized freedom and grasped it with alacrity when Yankee soldiers brought it within convenient reach. While the slaves waited for emancipation, they raised foodstuffs for civilians and soldiers, ran spinning wheels and looms on the plantations, worked in factories and mines, built fortifications, and served as nurses, cooks, and personal servants in the Southern army. Their good humor buoyed the spirits of white associates both at home and on the firing line. Their contribution to the Southern cause was enormous.

In the chapters that follow I have sketched the character and experiences of the Confederacy's humbler peoples—the Johnnies, the folk at home, and the Negroes. I have been conscious of a desire to give these plain folk a conspicuous place in the South's war history because of a long-standing conviction that they have not had due recognition. But at the same time I have striven earnestly to be objective.

In both form and content these essays are essentially as presented as the Fleming Lectures at Louisiana State University. I am indebted to Dr. Marcus M. Wilkerson, Director of the Louisiana State University Press, for assistance in preparing the manuscript for publications, and to Professor Edwin A. Davis for helpful suggestions concerning material and organization.

The Yale University Press and the Bobbs-Merrill Company generously permitted me to paraphrase and quote portions of two previous studies published, respectively, by them—*Southern Negroes, 1861–1865*, and *The Life of Johhny Reb: The Common Soldier of the Confederacy.*

BELL IRVIN WILEY

I

THE COMMON SOLDIERS

THE Southern Confederacy achieved her greatest renown from the exploits of her armed forces.
These forces were composed of two groups: the
officers and the common soldiers—the lowly men
who marched in the ranks and who by their con-
temporaries were given the sobriquet of Johnny
Rebs.[1]

The overwhelming majority of Rebs were
Southern-born, but a considerable sprinkling were
Yankees by birth; and the number who first saw
the light of day in foreign lands ran well up into
tens of thousands. Several regiments of red men
were organized in the Indian country, and in more
than one engagement the savage war whoop
blended with the Rebel yell to set Federal spines
a-tingling.

[1] Materials for this portrait of soldiers and soldier life are
drawn mainly from wartime letters and diaries, court-martial
records, muster rolls, medical reports, and other primary sources.

Well over half of those who wore the gray were tillers of the soil, but muster rolls list large numbers of students, laborers, clerks, mechanics, carpenters, merchants, blacksmiths, sailors, doctors, painters, teachers, shoemakers, lawyers, overseers, printers, masons, tailors, millers, coopers, and bakers. A sampling of 107 muster rolls representing seven states, 28 regiments and 9,000 private soldiers revealed more than 100 occupational groups ranging from apothecaries to wheelwrights, and including such surprising classifications as gamblers, rogues, and speculators.

Writers who treat the Confederate period in cursory fashion are prone to make much of the young boys and the old men who marched under the Stars and Bars. Both of these elements were represented, but in negligible proportions. Examination of descriptive rolls comprising 11,000 privates from eleven states recruited mainly in 1861–1862 revealed one 13-year-old boy and one 73-year-old man. Three recruits among the group were 14 years of age, 31 were 15, 200 were 16, and 366 were 17. Boys under 18 constituted approximately ½0 of the total; men in their 30's, ⅛; and those in their 40's, ½5. Eighty-six recruits fell in the 50–59 age group, 12 were 60–69, and one was 70. But ⅘ of the 11,000 cases were included within the limits of 18–29. Conscription acts passed in 1863 and 1864 doubtless changed somewhat the pattern represented by this sampling, but not enough to substantiate the charge made by Grant that the Confederacy robbed the cradle and the grave to sustain its armies. The overwhelming bulk of the Southern fighting force from beginning to end appears to have been made up of men ranging from 18 to 35.

Rebs were as diverse in culture and education as they were in age. Roseate reminiscers have had much to say of the gentle scholar who pored over his Greek and Latin books near the campfire, and there were some men of this type among the rank and file. But every learned Reb had several comrades who could not read or write at all. Company descriptive rolls which recruits were supposed to sign when they were mustered into service afford some idea of the extent of illiteracy. In a few companies more than half of the privates had to make x marks in the spaces allotted to signatures; and almost every company had from one to a score of men who could not sign their names. But the majority of Rebs had sufficient education to enable them to write letters to their home folk, though usually not without mighty struggles with spelling, grammar, and chirography.

The bulk of the Confederacy's fighting forces came from nonslaveholding families. In a general way they reflected both the weaknesses and the virtues of the yeoman society from which they sprang. They were naïve, susceptible to prejudice, neglectful of sanitation, haphazard in dress, and unpolished in manner; but they were endowed with a good measure of integrity, self-respect, and courage.

One of the principal concerns of Johnny Rebs, whatever their economic or cultural status, was food. In the early days of the war, rations were generally adequate, and some of the volunteers fared sumptuously. Government issues of beef, oven-baked bread, and vegetables were supplemented by all sorts of delicacies sent from home or brought in by patriotic citizens living near the camps.

But the days of abundance were short. In 1862 a general diminution of the government ration became necessary, and further curtailments were ordered in 1863 and 1864. The deterioration of transportation facilities restricted the flow of supplies from home to a mere trickle. Except in camps that were close to food-producing areas, full stomachs were the exception rather than the rule after 1862.

In some instances acute deprivation came early in the war. During the retrograde movement from Yorktown to Richmond in the spring of 1862, some of Daniel H. Hill's men subsisted for three days on dry corn issued in the shuck and shelled and parched by the men. "I have never conceived of such trials as we passed through," wrote one soldier after this retreat; and another observed, "I came nearer starving than I ever did before."

Hunger was more common during periods of active campaigning, particularly when forced marches were the order of the day. Suffering was acute in the rapid withdrawals from Antietam in 1862, from Gettysburg in 1863, and from Petersburg in 1865. The nadir of deprivation was experienced by soldiers under siege at Port Hudson and Vicksburg—where dwindling larders caused resort to such expedients as peabread, boiled weeds, stewed rat, and roasted mule.

The mainstays of diet after the first year of war were cornbread and meat, and of these the Rebs became exceedingly tired. "If the war closes and I get to come home I never intend to chew

[5]

any more cornbread," wrote a Mississippian in 1863; and about the same time a comrade scribbled poetically in his diary:

Oh what a wonderful day is this
When our rations a little more than meal do consist,
I'd give a great deal for some turkey or Beef
To comfort our stomachs and give them relief.

Just prior to Lee's surrender a Louisianian said: "If any person offers me cornbread after this war comes to a close I shall *probably* tell him to— go to hell." But the quality of meat elicited even more eloquent disparagement. "The beef is so poor it is Sticky and Blue," observed Private O. T. Hanks; "if a quarter was thrown against the wall it would stick." Another Reb complained that the cows which supplied the meat for his regiment were so emaciated that "it takes two hands to hold up one beef to shoot it."

Experience proved to the majority of Johnnies that they could live and fight on the most meager rations, but they never ceased yearning for the abundance of home larders. Through their letters they kept a close tab on fruits and vegetables as they came into season, and hog-killing time almost invariably evoked expressions of homesickness and war-weariness.

Some soldiers made unreasonable demands upon their home folk. A hungry North Carolinian wrote in the fall of 1864:

Dear Father I want that Box you loud to send to me I want sweet Bread and pyes and Cab'g heads and all you think nesery and some of that strong stuff its a little like camfire all it lacks the camfire ant in it But it drinkes all write aney way you can give a ruf ges what it is and Send me some money if you please . . . and I want you to send me some paper two and send me some red peper and some unions and Butter and evything that you can think of appels two for I had forgot the apples and some eggs and potatoes iresh potatoes and sweet ones and Biskets and I want you to send me a Jacket and gloves and two pare of sox and dont fail Dear father I must clos as I hant got much to write[.]

A Texan, who suffered exceedingly from the failure of Bragg's commissariat at Chattanooga, reflected a widespread sentiment when he said that if he ever got back to his father's house he intended "to take a hundred biscuit and two large hams call it three days rations, then go down on Goat Island and eat it all at ONE MEAL."

Experiences as to clothing were much like those

concerning food. Army regulations of 1861 prescribed natty outfits consisting of gray tunics, sky-blue trousers, double-breasted gray overcoats fitted with capes, French-style caps with havelocks of canvas or oilcloth to protect the neck, black leather cravats, and Jefferson-style boots. These specifications were reissued year after year, but they received scant attention in actual practice. The sky-blue trousers seem to have been exceptional even in 1861, and no mention of them is found after the first year of the war, except in army regulations. The tunic soon gave way to a short jacket which came to have such universal use as to cause the application of the name "gray jackets" to the generality of soldiers. A soft felt hat replaced the kepi as a headpiece, and brogan shoes were substituted for the Jefferson boots.

Early in the war there was much display of finery. In 1861 the Georgia Hussars left Savannah in resplendent uniforms costing in the aggregate some $25,000. The Orleans Guard Battalion wore flashy blue dress uniforms, dating back to militia parade occasions, into the action at Shiloh. Fellow soldiers mistook the blue-garbed Louisianians for Yankees and began to shoot at them. The Guards forestalled annihilation by quickly turning their coats inside out so as to present the white linings, and thus they went through the fight. Other volunteer outfits arrived at the front in uniforms of green, yellow, and flaming red. Most outlandish of all were the uniforms worn by the notorious Louisiana Zouaves; these consisted of scarlet bloomers, blue shirts, brocaded jackets, wide sashes, white gaiters, and gaudy fezzes worn at a jaunty angle.

Fine uniforms were as short-lived as sumptuous rations. By 1863 Confederate gray had given way in large measure to a rough fabric made in Southern mills or in home looms, and dyed with a native coloring made of walnut hulls and copperas. The yellowish hue of suits made from this cloth fastened upon Johnny Rebs a title that gained wide use in both North and South; namely that of "butternuts." By 1864 butternut jackets and blue trousers taken from dead Yankees on the battlefield had become a sort of unofficial standard of what the well-dressed Reb should wear.

But in spite of Yankee providence and the utmost exertions of home folk and government purchasing agents, Rebel wardrobes were never adequate. The most acute shortages were those of shoes and blankets. Experiments were made with shoes fashioned about the campfire from raw-hides secured at army slaughter pens, but these expedients proved unsatisfactory.

Johnnies attempted to rehabilitate their uniforms with needle and thread, but maladroit seamsters "puckered" their patches, and strenuous campaigning caused wear to outstrip repair. In June, 1864, a Texan summed up with striking aptness the Rebel clothing situation. "In this army," he wrote from near Atlanta, "one hole in the seat of the breeches indicates a captain, two holes a lieutenant, and the seat of the pants all out indicates that the individual is a private."

Confederate soldiers had many other woes besides hunger and raggedness. In summer the flies, mosquitoes, and gnats that swarmed about encampments made life utterly miserable. Body lice gnawed away without regard to season. "There is not a man in the army, officer or private that does not have from a Battalion to a Brigade of Body lice on him," wrote one Reb in 1863; and others dubbed the pests with such military names as "graybacks," "Zouaves," "tigers," and "Bragg's body-guard." Killing lice was referred to as fighting under the black flag; throwing away an infested shirt was called giving the vermin a parole; and evading them by turning a garment wrong side out became "the execution of a flank movement." One sardonic Reb when about to go to bed was seen to assume a prayerful pose and to recite:

> Now I lay me down to sleep,
> While gray-backs o'er my body creep;
> If I should die before I wake,
> I pray the Lord their jaws to break.

Disease was an inevitable concomitant of the hunger, the exposure, the filth, and the vermin which bedeviled Confederates. The first malady to strike in epidemic proportions was measles. In one camp of 10,000 recruits, 4,000 men were stricken; and during the first year of war the percentage of illness was heavy throughout the army. Comparatively few men died from measles alone, but mortality from subsequent complications was heavy. A prevalent attitude was reflected by a Reb who wrote in July, 1861: "I had rather risk my life in battle than with the measles in camp."

Dysentery and diarrhea were an exceedingly great scourge. One soldier observed: "it is a very rare thing to find a man in this army who has not got the diorreah." And reliable medical records tend to sustain his observation.

Malaria, typhoid, smallpox, pneumonia, scurvy, and pulmonary tuberculosis each took a considerable toll from Rebel ranks. One private remarked in 1862 that "Big Battles is not as Bad as the fever." And a prominent Confederate doctor who made a careful study of medical records after the war estimated that for every soldier who died as a result of battle there were three who perished from disease.

Much of the mortality from sickness was due to the undeveloped state of medical practice which prevailed during Civil War times. Inadequacy of medicine and hospital facilities also had a part in the tragedy. Scarcity of well-trained doctors was a further cause. One poor Reb complained that "Doctors kills more than they cour. . . . Doctors haint Got half Sence." And there were enough quacks among army practitioners to lend considerable credence to his charge.

Among lesser woes of the rank and file were the incompetency and highhandedness of officers. This gave rise to numerous difficulties between officers and soldiers. Some of the conflict with superiors derived from the soldiers' misconception of military usages. The authoritative manner in which officers gave orders was viewed by some privates as a personal insult, and therefore deeply resented. Other Rebs were aggrieved by alleged discrimination as to the assignment of guard and fatigue duty, and the granting of furloughs. "I am not allowed the chance of a dog," bemoaned a Texan in 1863. "Col Young . . . can go to Hell for my part you know that if any one will try to do I can get along with them but when they get Hell in their Neck I cant do any thing . . . and so I dont try . . . he has acted the dam dog and I cant tell him so if I do they will put me in the Guard House . . . but I can tell him what I think of him when this war ends."

Many of the disparaging statements of privates concerning their superiors were exaggerated, but there can be no doubt that the Confederacy had its share of incompetent officers. Sometimes, sorely tried Rebs took upon themselves the responsibility of putting offensive superiors in their places. Privates of the Fifty-third Georgia Regiment rode their colonel on a rail and thus extracted from him the promise to treat them more civilly—and the colonel submitted contritely to this treatment. A Tarheel wrote in 1862 concerning his captain: "he put me in the gard house one time & he got drunk agoin from Wilmington to Golesboro on the train and we put him in the Sh-t House so we are even."

The most despicable of all the officers were those who showed the white feather under fire. An illuminating glimpse of the disdain in which such leaders were held is afforded by the following entry in a Reb's diary:

Camp Vandorn Agust 5 1862
The following little piece of poitry made its appearance in camp to day a little explainnation will be nessary to understand it right it is got up on Leueit Doyle of the Franklin Lilf [?] guards who did not stand fire at the James Island Fight on the 16th of June and as gained some notoriety for putting the Boys in the Guard House for not walking there post on Guard when he is Officer of the Guard he putts on a great many airs and is disliked by the Boys Generly he used to cause a good deal of amusement when he was a Drilling his company with his hand grasp around the hilt of his sword and the blade parallel with the ground he would command them to left wheal, with all the cautionary remarks such as steady; steady; on the pivot come round like a gate now. hepp. hepp. and so on. The Fort Doyle that is spoking of is the

Boys that he had put in the Guard House gathered
up some old camp kettels and mounted them in
front of the Guard House calling the fort after
him[.]

Latest From The War;

The last Fight at Secessionville!

We went to Secessionville a disturbance to quell
Where the Yankees were storming our batteries,
    in fact raising hell
The boys all pitched in as all who are brave
Not one of them flinching not one of them caved

Except one—Mr. Doyal who stopped when he
    saw
Shot falling so fast—for want of sand in [h]is
    craw
He turned on his pivot—swung around like a gate
And made strides from the field from six feet to
    eight

He left in a hurry, and we all really suppose
His time is the fastest on record—yet nobody
    knows
He went to the Surgeon and struck for a job
To act as assistant, or be placed in a squad

The Surgeon was busy, and made no reply
So Doyal left the line another place to try

He left swift footed, and we saw him no more
Untill the day was far spent, and the battle was oer

When he again turned on his pivot, swung around
    like a gate
Walked into supper—sat down and ate
So in honor of him, we've erected Fort Doyal
Costing large sums of money—besides great toil
       A gun shall be fired at the raising of each
        sun
          In honor of Doyal, who at Secessionville
        run

Now listen to me, take the advice of a friend
Be true to the country, you've taken arms to de-
    fend,
Let your motto be onward and go straight ahead
Though you march through blood and crawl oer
    the dead

So on ward it is dont flinch "nary" time
Glory, honor, and victory, shall surely be thine
Be kind to the boys, and treat them all well
Or they'll blow up the Fort—and send you to hell.
                    Patriotic

One of the most trying phases of soldier life
was the drabness of camp routine. Country-bred
Rebs, accustomed to the freedom of farm and
forest, were exceedingly irked by the endless re-

currence of reveille, roll call, drill, and retreat. Even more intolerable were the periodic turns at guard duty. "Oh how glad I will be when the day comes that we . . . never hear the Tap of a drum again which bids us to rise and drill," wrote a Mississippian in 1863; and a comrade blurted: "When this war is over I will whip the man that says 'fall in' to me."

From the devious ills that oppressed them, Rebs naturally sought sundry escapes. Some lightened the load of boredom by reading, but this diversion was greatly restricted by the scarcity of books and papers, the inadequacy of lighting facilities, and, except during winter quarters, by the interposition of camp duties. Many soldiers found keen enjoyment in swimming, fishing, hunting, baseball, wrestling, foot racing, marbles, and tenpins—the last played by rolling cannon balls at holes in the ground.

Music was the most popular form of diversion. Soldiers gathered about the campfire or in winter huts to sing such wartime favorites as "Home Sweet Home," "Lorena," "Annie Laurie," "Juanita," "Sweet Evelena," "When This Cruel War is Over," and a lugubrious number borrowed from the Yankees which had the title, "Just Before the Battle, Mother." Regimental bands gave occasional concerts, but Rebs enjoyed more the informal "jam sessions" at which small groups of fiddlers and guitarists "cut loose" on such tunes as "Dixie," "Hell Broke Loose in Georgia," "Willie's on the Dark Blue Sea," "Arkansas Traveller," "When I Saw Sweet Nellie Home," and "Oh Lord Gals One Friday."

Theatricals, womanless dances, parties at country houses near the camps, and visits to cities provided occasional breaks in camp routine. A few outfits, such as Morgan's cavalry and Price's Missourians, printed camp newspapers on cherished presses that were hauled about the countryside. Less fortunate units occasionally issued small newssheets done entirely with pens.

Pranks and teasing afforded diversion for countless Rebs. One group of veterans "honored" a greenhorn recruit by electing him to the fictitious position of fifth lieutenant. When the novice inquired in all seriousness as to the duties of his office he was told that they consisted of carrying water and catching fleas out of the soldiers' beds. He actually attempted to discharge these responsibilities until some generous comrade revealed the hoax to him.

The appearance in camp of a soldier or civilian wearing any sort of unusual garb would elicit a chorus of jibes and taunts. If the visitor was a little man wearing high boots the cry would be, "Come up out of them thar boots; I know you're in thar; I see your arms sticking out." A characteristic greeting for a man with a "stovepipe" headpiece was: "Come out of that hat; I see your legs"; or, "Look out, that parrot shell you're wearing's going to explode"; or, "Take that camp kettle home. Aren't you ashamed to steal a poor soldier's camp kettle?"

A staff officer who rode through camp sporting a finely twisted mustache was almost certain to receive from behind tents and stumps the irreverent suggestion: "Take them mice out'er your mouth; take em out; no use to say they aint thar; see their tails hangin' out." An enormous beard might elicit the suggestion: "Come out er that bunch of har. I see your ears a workin'."

If some soldier happened to mimic a chicken, a cow, or a donkey the whole camp would break out in a chorus of cackling, crowing, shooing, braying, or bellowing. When a Reb on the march greeted a friend with "How are you, Jim?" fellow soldiers would follow suit until Jim was overwhelmed with the greetings of a brigade or division.

Rebs sometimes purloined one another's letters. Discovery of a sugary missive from some indiscreet sweetheart would immediately lead to a broadcasting of the contents and the taunting of the recipient. Private J. W. Rabb one day received a poetically endearing letter from his sister Bet. When this note was discovered by Rabb's comrades they jumped to the conclusion that Bet was his sweetheart; and they proceeded to tease him roundly. Rabb's barely decipherable narration of this incident to his sister gives a significant insight into the bantering, fun-loving character of the common soldier: "You roate me such a good long letter," he observed. "i like it so much for the boys all thought that it was from my jularky and one little fellow develed me so much about Fly home to thy native home gentle dove he sayed that I looked more like a paterage."

Excursions through the countryside in search of supplies afforded diversion for many soldiers. Much of this foraging was of the innocent sort, but an objective study of primary sources makes inescapable the conclusion that theft and destruction of private property were also woefully common among wearers of the gray. Early in 1862 the practice of stealing rails for campfires became so prevalent that the Secretary of War issued a circular stating that "unless the destruction of fences can be arrested it will materially lessen the crop . . . and impair the power of the Government to subsist the Army." Prohibitive orders against this evil were promulgated repeatedly, but they were of little avail. By the spring of 1865 a rail fence in an area near Confederate camps was a rare spectacle.

Theft of hogs and poultry was even more common than molestation of premises. A pig that made the mistake of wandering near an encampment had small chance of survival. Soldiers throughout the army enjoyed a story that ran something like this: One day a Reb came to camp with a bulging object concealed under his coat. On being questioned by a lieutenant as to the nature of his burden he replied, "It's a pig." When the officer inquired if he was not aware of the stringent orders against shooting livestock, he responded, "Yes, sir, I know it's against regulations, but I killed this pig in self-defense."

"But how was that?" asked the officer.

"Well," responded the culprit, "I was coming

up the path back yonder when I heard something roaring behind me. I looked around and saw a pig coming out of a hole in the ground. Just before it got to me I fired, and it was mortally wounded."

Whereupon, according to the tale, the officer appropriated the meat to his own use.

No doubt many pillagers were influenced by a feeling that the country for which they were fighting owed them sustenance, and that if the commissariat did not furnish them with an adequate supply of edibles, there was no harm in providing for themselves. This point of view was reflected by the statement of a Reb who observed to his brother in 1863: "The Government tries to feed us Texains on Poor Beef, but there is too Dam many hogs here for that, these Arkansaw hoosiers ask from 25 to 30 cents a pound for there pork, but the boys generally get it a little *cheaper than that.* I reckon you understand how they get it."

Gardens, orchards, smokehouses, and beehives were likewise plundered by Confederates. On June 2, 1864, a soldier wrote to his wife from a camp in North Mississippi: "Our soldiers act outrageously . . . in reference to . . . private property. . . . [They] have not left a fat hog, chicken, Turkey, goose, duck, or eggs, or onions behind." Other troops wrote their home folk that a visitation of Rebels was to be dreaded almost as much as invasion by the Federals. A Georgian addressing his wife in July, 1864, sized up the situation thus: "I have but little or no fears that the Yanks will ever git down to whare you are but I think you will be pesterde by our own soldiers . . . strowling about . . . and stealing your chickens, etc. I had almost as leave have the Yankees around my hous as our own men, except they will not insult ladies."

Much has been said by descendants of Confederates about the good conduct of Rebels who invaded Pennsylvania in 1863. But letters written at the time by men who participated in the campaign do not square with Lee's published order against molestation of enemy property. An army doctor recorded in his diary while at Chambersburg that "hogs, sheep, and Poultries stand a poor chance about here for their lives," and added significantly, "we are living on the 'fat of the land.'" A Virginia officer reported to his family about the same time that Southern soldiers "took everything" from farmers along the line of march; "they even stripped their houses," he added, "though it was against orders." Still another officer observed: "It seems to do the men good to burn Yankee rails as they have not left a fence in our part of the country. . . . In spite of orders they slip out at night and help themselves to milk, butter, poultry, and vegetables."

A considerable number of Rebs sought surcease from the humdrum of camp life in lurid associations, for the Confederate Army, like all other large military organizations, was bedeviled by prostitutes. Some "fancy women" plied their vocations by donning masculine attire and joining up as soldiers. Others set up establishments in communities adjoining encampments. In the spring of 1864 one of Joe Johnston's staff officers wrote to the post commander at Dalton, Georgia: "Complaints are daily made to me of the number of lewd women in this town, and on the outskirts of the army. They are said to be impregnating this whole command, and the Commissariat has been frequently robbed with a view of supporting these disreputable characters." The vice situation in this area became so serious that General Johnston issued an order to have the town and the surrounding country searched, so that all women who were not able to give proof of respectability and the means of an honest livelihood might be sent to points beyond the reach of his soldiers. But in view of prior failures, it is doubtful if this measure met with much success.

Richmond and Petersburg, because of their proximity to large troop concentrations, became veritable meccas for *"nymphes du monde,"* and soldiers on leave flocked to their houses by the score. The sad story of this allurement is told on monthly regimental sick reports, many of which are on file in The National Archives. One regiment of about a thousand men, which moved from rural Alabama to Richmond for a few weeks' sojourn in the summer of 1861, reported for the month of July sixty-two new cases of gonorrhea and six of syphilis.

Perhaps the most pervasive of unorthodox diversions was gambling. Cards—some of them bearing the likeness of Jefferson Davis—dice, chuck-a-luck banks, and raffling boards were everywhere in evidence on payday. Even the lice that swarmed the camps were pitted against each other at trials of speed, with tin plates, canteen sides, or small circles inscribed on tent flies constituting the race tracks. In December, 1862, shortly after a visit of the paymaster, Private Ruffin Thomson wrote to his mother: "Yesterday was Sunday and I sat at my fire and saw the preachers holding forth about thirty steps off, and between them and me were two games of poker, where each one was trying to fill his pockets at the expense of his neighbor. Chuck-a-luck and faro banks are running night and day with eager and excited crowds standing around with their hands full of money. Open gambling has been prohibited, but that amounts to nothing."

Drinking was almost as pervasive as gambling. A chaplain testified that after First Manassas "drunkenness became so common as to scarcely excite remark, and many men who were temperate . . . at home fell into the delusion that drinking was excusable, if not necessary, in the army." Ministers threatened tipplers repeatedly with hell-fire, and commanding generals showered them with punishments, but to little avail. Thirsty Rebs were ingenious at devising means of "flanking" prohibitions, and rare were the times when some sort of "distilled damnation" was not procurable. The potency of Confederate liquor, as well as the esteem in which it was held, was reflected by nicknames applied to it by campaign-hardened butternuts; among the appellations were these: "How Come You So," "Tanglefoot," "Rifle Knock-

Knee," "Bust Skull," "Old Red Eye," and "Rock
Me To Sleep, Mother."

While some Rebs were seeking relief from
hardship and ennui in worldly pleasures, others
were finding solace in religion. In fact, the violent
encounters on the battlefield were matched
throughout by conflicts no less mighty within
Rebel ranks between the forces of sin and those
of righteousness. And at war's end, it must have
seemed to many Southerners that Mammon had
won a decisive victory in both contests.

In the early days of the war, chaplains made
but little progress in religious undertakings. Soldiers seemed obsessed with the idea of having a
fling at evil while absence from home restraints
—which absence they thought would be ended
shortly by overwhelming Southern victory—afforded the opportunity. Many divines despaired
after a few months of fruitless endeavor and returned to their homes.

But more persistent church authorities worked
on. Agents were sent abroad to purchase Bibles,
while at home tract societies were organized to
publish Testaments and religious pamphlets. Col-
porteurs and chaplains fairly flooded camps with
the literature thus obtained.

By the autumn of 1863 the evangelistic efforts of the various denominations were in full swing. By that time also soldier attitudes toward religion had become more receptive. The reverses of Gettysburg and Vicksburg dispelled what little there remained of hope for a short war. Dwindling of regiments from hundreds to scores impressed upon survivors the uncertainty of life. The prospect of conflicts in the future, even more deadly than those of the past, was a powerful incentive for accepting the chaplain's promise of heavenly bliss to those who would renounce sin.

These and other influences led in the fall of 1863 to an army-wide outburst of revivals. Prominent ministers—eager to exchange indifferent home congregations for enthusiastic hearers in the army—flocked to camp to give gray-clad penitents the benefits of their fervid oratory. Stonewall Jackson and other spiritually-concerned generals suspended drill to accommodate day services, and at night encampments reverberated with the prayers and the hymns of both seekers and Christians.

The high tide of revivalism extended through the winter, but renewal of active campaigning in the spring of 1864 restricted the religious program. Converts absorbed in marching and fighting naturally neglected their Bibles and prayers. Backsliding became rife, and standby evils of swearing, drinking, and gambling emerged from eclipse.

The war's last winter saw the recurrence of large-scale revivals, but the peak of the previous year was not regained.

Most commanding officers attributed to religion a salutary effect on morale. Granting the general correctness of this view, it was unfortunate for the Confederacy that army revivals moved only a minority to repentance, and that evangelistic influences were so often ephemeral.

For morale sank to a very low ebb during the latter half of the war. The initial wave of patriotism that swept over the Confederacy after Fort Sumter was not of long duration. War-weariness began to creep into home letters after a few months, and discontent gained momentum during the dull period of hibernation. The Conscription Act of April, 1862, compelling to further service men whose terms of voluntary enlistment were about to expire, was a severe blow to morale. The victories of summer and autumn aroused lagging spirits for a time, but the reverses of Gettysburg and Vicksburg the following year brought unprecedented gloom. There was some improvement in the spring of 1864 when Grant bogged down in the Wilderness, but Sherman's march through the heart of the Confederacy and Hood's disaster in Tennessee gave new impetus to defeatism.

Many Rebs who might have remained firm in the face of repeated reverses on the field of battle had their spirits broken by the reports of hunger, raggedness, and sickness that came to them from loved ones at home. An Alabaman who received a distressing letter from his wife wrote back that he was going to ask immediately for a furlough, but that if his request for leave was rejected, he was "coming home enny how . . . for I cant stand to here that you and the children are Sufren for Bread."

Declining morale was evidenced by a mounting tide of leave-taking. Some of the men who slipped away from camp under cover of night went home to harvest the crop, to cut the winter's supply of wood, to tan the leather for shoes, or to bury a dead child, and then returned voluntarily to camp. But a much larger number took to fastnesses of mountain and forest and flaunted Confederate authority for the duration of the war.

All in all, more than one hundred thousand men swelled the roll of deserters.

Military authorities might have stemmed the tide of leave-taking by a more consistent meting of severe penalties. Unwarranted absences of short duration were often unpunished, and in many other cases offenders received such trivial sentences as reprimand by a company officer, digging a stump, carrying a rail for an hour or two, wearing a placard inscribed with the letters AWOL, confinement in the guardhouse, marching about camp in a barrel shirt, riding a wooden horse, and marking time on the head of a molasses keg.

Punishments for desertion were considerably more severe than those for absence without leave. Burning the letter *D* on hip or hand with a red-hot iron and then drumming the delinquent out of camp to the tune of "Yankee Doodle" or the "rogue's march" was a favorite sentence of some courts-martial. Before enactment of an interdicting law in April, 1863, whipping was a common punishment for deserters. Another corrective in fairly common use was head shaving, followed by long imprisonment at hard labor with ball and chain. But some courts prescribed such lenient sen-

[31]

tences as forfeiture of a few months' pay, or the carrying of weights on the parade ground.

Tribunals showed the greatest reluctance to impose the death sentence, and if execution was prescribed, there was considerable likelihood of interposition by higher authorities. In 245 cases of conviction for desertion during the last six months of the war by courts belonging mainly to Lee's army, the death sentence was ordered in only 70 instances, and 31 of these sentences were invalidated by President Davis' general amnesty of February, 1865. Others were probably set aside by Lee and Joseph E. Johnston.

But during the course of the war many deserters paid the supreme penalty. When time came for the execution, the culprits were usually mounted on their coffins, taken to a hollow square, and shot as they knelt beside open graves. Comrades forced to witness these gruesome ceremonies were greatly awed. But the realization that scores deserted with impunity for every one that was shot must have left an impression more enduring even than the ghastliness of execution.

Great as was the tide of desertion and leave-taking, the majority of Rebs stayed at their posts till death, disability, or peace gave them honorable discharge. But the morale of many of these faithful ones wavered. There were times when the manifest selfishness, bickering, and inefficiency drove them near the point of desperation, but family pride, an inner sense of honor, or motives less worthy, restrained them.

The spirit of the youngsters was much better than that of their older comrades. They could wade through a sea of blood one day and snap back to cheerfulness the next. They bore the strain of marching, the inclemencies of weather, the scourge of disease, the scantiness of rations, and the separation from loved ones with much greater equanimity than did men in the thirties and forties who had wives, children, and other home responsibilities. The older men let their minds dwell unduly on the horrors of battle. They weighted their spirits by taking thought of the morrow. They appropriated the gloom of their home folk. They were crushed by longing for wives and children. And when sick or wounded they were apt to grovel in despair. If the Confederate War gave any formula for happy soldierhood, it was this: "Be young and unattached."

But what of the conduct of Rebs on the battlefield? Space will not permit a full answer to this question, but it should be said in this connection that the Confederate army like all other large military organizations was cursed with numerous cowards. Every sizable encounter from Bull Run to Bentonville had its portion of skulkers and shirkers. And there were times of panic, as at Missionary Ridge in 1863 and at Winchester and Cedar Creek in 1864, when entire regiments and brigades broke under attack and gave themselves to shameful flight. After Cedar Hill, General Bryan Grimes wrote: "It was the hardest day's work I ever engaged in trying to rally the men. Took over flags at different times, begging, commanding, entreating the men to rally—would ride up and down the lines, beseeching them by all they held sacred and dear to stop and fight but without any success. I dont mean my brigade only, but all." And a captain who witnessed the rout at Winchester wrote: "The Ladies of Winchester came into the streets and beged them crying bitterly to make a stand for their sakes if not for their own honor, but to no avail. The cowards did not have the shame to make a pretense of halting."

But taken as a whole the fighting record of the men who wore the gray was a good one. On dozens of battlefields humble men from the Southern hinterland rose to great heights of individual valor and transformed their tattered butternut uniforms into emblems of glory. The world has known no better fighters than the yelling Southern hosts who charged the heights at Malvern Hill and at Gettysburg.

And even in defeat the spirit of some remained indomitable. A few years ago when this writer visited relatives near Pulaski, Tennessee, he was escorted to New Zion churchyard to see the grave of a Confederate veteran named Tom Doss. The grave lies north and south with the headstone at the south. This unorthodox arrangement was of Tom's own planning. Shortly before he died he made his family promise that they would bury him with his feet to the north, so that when Gabriel blew the trumpet on the morn of resurrection he would be in a convenient position to give the Yankees a resounding kick.

II

THE FOLK AT HOME

THE humble white folk constituted the great
bulk of the Confederacy's civilian populace, just
as they made up the lion's share of her fighting
force. Most of these lowly people lived on the
farm in small ill-furnished houses. A majority
owned plots of land ranging from a few acres to
a quarter section; a negligible proportion possessed from one to a half dozen slaves. They were
sparsely educated and generally rough in appearance and demeanor. Some were so shiftless, ignorant, undernourished, and depraved as to merit
the title of "poor white trash," but the great
majority compared favorably with the planter
class in self-respect, in integrity, and in the other
attributes of character and citizenship.

The war affected the life of the lower classes
in many ways. Particularly vital was its influence

on food. In 1861 there was little change in either the quantity or quality of edibles. But from 1862 on, impingements came in increasing number and weight.

One of the first items to be dropped from the dietary list was coffee. By no means all of the humbler folk had been accustomed to this beverage in ante-bellum times, but those who had enjoyed their regular morning cup felt the deprivation keenly. Various substitutes were utilized, including parched particles of sweet potatoes, peanuts, rye, corn, English peas, and okra; some users boasted that the improvisations were almost as satisfying as the genuine Rio, but most of these testimonials savored more of patriotism than of sincerity.

Except in Louisiana and southern Mississippi, sugar became so dear after the first year of the war as to be rarely obtainable by the poorer classes. Sorghum cane, grown before the war only in limited quantities, was planted extensively throughout the Confederacy, and sorghum molasses became a universal sweetener for "ersatz" coffee, and for pies, cakes, and gingerbread. Honey was also a widely used substitute for sugar. A few enterprising housewives made sirup from watermelon juice, but the great majority deemed this process impracticable.

Peanuts—known also as pindars, goobers, and ground peas—were roasted and eaten about the fireside or mixed with molasses to make nourishing candy. Poultry and dairy products were enjoyed to only a limited extent except by the more thrifty. In most localities fruits and vegetables were abundant in season, and provident households dried large quantities of apples and peaches for use during the winter. But the staple items of diet were sweet potatoes, common field peas, bread, molasses, and meat. Most of the bread was made of corn meal, for wheat was scarce except in a few localities. Meat consisted mainly of salted or pickled pork.

The majority of humble folk seem to have had enough food throughout the Confederate period to forestall the pains of hunger. Some, indeed, fared better during the war than before, thanks to the legislative curtailment of cotton and tobacco. But there were thousands of instances of deprivation. Suffering was most frequent in areas lying within reach of either the Federal or the Confederate army and in sections inhabited mainly by nonslaveholders. Tenant classes in the

country and wage earners of town and city experienced greater hardship than did people of
higher economic standing. Those who owned slaves
suffered least of all.

Shortage of manpower was a paramount factor
in the scarcity of food. In countless instances conscription took away all the adult males of a household, and in some cases entire communities were
stripped of the accustomed food producers.
Women, children, and older men assumed the full
responsibility of farming, and some achieved notable success. But planting and harvesting operations
were too onerous for the majority. Women with
small children had little time for field work.

Visits by husbands or sons in the army afforded
some respite, but these furloughs as often as not
resulted in the addition of new members to the
household, thus enhancing rather than abating
the problem of subsistence.

The question naturally arises: what of the labor
of the multiplied thousands of men who evaded
military service? Comparatively few of those who
escaped the army by exemption, substitution, or
detail belonged to the farmer class; and the majority of those who deserted found it difficult to
tend their crops with any degree of regularity

because of the threatened visitation of enrolling officers. It must be admitted, however, that many cases of hunger were prevented by the irrepressible practice of Rebs absenting themselves without leave during the planting and harvesting season.

Pertinent likewise to the hunger experienced by home folk was the deficiency of livestock and farm equipment. In many instances horses and mules were taken by military authorities or by guerrillas, and it was almost impossible to replace work animals lost to use for any reason. Plows, wagons, hoes, scythes, and cane grinders incapacitated by wear or by breakage frequently had to remain idle for months because of the owner's inability to procure new parts or to engage the services of a blacksmith. In the latter part of the war many poor families were reduced to such archaic expedients as threshing their wheat by beating the heads over barrels, and then winnowing it in the breezes.

Scarcity of salt militated against preservation of meat, and the difficulty of procuring jars complicated the problem of canning fruits and vegetables. But these factors were less responsible for the hunger which cursed the Confederacy than

were the companion evils of inflation and speculation. Constantly soaring prices caused producers
to hoard their crops, and from 1862 until the end
of the war the South was beset with a speculation
mania. Men left the army in large numbers to
join a host of entrepreneurs already engaged in
buying corn, wheat, salt, meat, molasses, whisky,
and cotton cards, and holding them until scarcity
and inflation made possible a trebling of their investments. Many producers and speculators refused to sell at all for Confederate money, but
demanded specie—which simply was not to be
had by the lower classes; or they required barter
for articles that were even dearer than those offered in exchange.

Against this tide of profiteering there was little
chance for the poor, particularly for women who
depended for a livelihood mainly upon the eleven
dollars a month drawn by their soldier husbands
from a government that was always in arrears
with its obligations. Private and public agencies
attempted to remedy this deplorable situation by
dispensing money and supplies. Voluntary relief
associations of towns and cities staged fairs,
bazaars, pantomimes, and tableaux to support free
markets for the poor.

In North Carolina county governments raised no less than twenty million dollars for the relief of soldiers' families, and the state contributed several million dollars more. In Alabama, and in other states as well, taxes were suspended in invaded areas, and salt was given to the needy. The Louisiana legislature authorized the governor in 1864 to purchase corn, bacon, flour, sugar, and beef for distribution in districts where provisions were unusually scarce. In many instances public-spirited individuals looked after the needs of indigent soldier families of their neighborhoods. One North Carolinian who owned a gristmill ground corn without toll; another donated grain to forty families. A third assumed the responsibility of sustaining twenty-five impoverished families for several months. In all parts of the Confederacy there were occasional philanthropists who sold corn and wheat to soldiers' wives at figures far below the current price.

But relief measures both public and private fell far short of the needs. Appropriations were inadequate and local committees who bore the brunt of relief administration were frequently incompetent or negligent. A North Carolina county court clerk wrote to Governor Zebulon B. Vance in

1863: "I feel it my duty to report to you the dereliction of the magistrates . . . with regard to our volunteers' families. They are actually suffering and I have made four unsuccessful attempts to get a quorum and have failed every time. . . . How can our soldiers fight when they know that their wives and children are destitute of even a peace of bread?" The relief money, allocated on a per capita basis, was nearly always incommensurate with the high prices that had to be paid for provisions. Frequently the recipients could find no one who would sell to them even though they trudged for miles about the countryside. And if they were successful in buying corn or wheat they often had no means of transporting it to their homes.

Red tape was also an omnipresent deterrent to the relief program. In North Carolina soldiers' wives who lived in a county other than that from which their husbands enlisted were not entitled to assistance. Dependents of substitutes were denied public support. Frequently, no provision was made for the help of families who had no immediate relative in military service.

A graphic picture of the deprivation and hunger suffered by the wives and mothers of the poorest soldiers is afforded by letters written to Governor Vance. Vance, by his democratic manner and his oft-expressed concern for his humble constituents, elicited an unusual amount of correspondence from them. Some of the complaints are obviously exaggerated, but others have an unmistakable ring of sincerity. One woman, who wanted her son furloughed to help with the harvest, wrote thus:

"Der Mr Vance i wante you if you plese you and Mr Davis to fix preperashenes to send home the poer solgers to cut the wheat for we have soad aboute fiftween bushel . . . excepten you gentlemen fixes sum way fer ous we can not get it cut . . . i hope that you and Mr Davis will helpe ous all you can fer yous are all the wones that can dew aney thing."

Another who had tried without success to buy wheat wrote: "them that has to Sell wont sell . . . tha will hafto bee Some amands made or the soldiers wifes will Starve. D. H. Peeler raisd a hundred an two bushels of wheat an wont Sell. John Mull raised hundred and 9 bushels . . . and wont Sell he is a welthy man. . . . Missis feeler a widow woman rais 94 . . . bushel of wheat an wont sell."

A third poured out her woes *in extenso:* "governer Vance i set down to rite you afew lins and pray to god that you will oblige me i ame apore woman with a posel of little children and i wil hav to starv or go neked me and my little children if my husban is kep a way from home much longer . . . i beg you to let him come tha dont give me but thre dolars a month and fore of us in famely . . . i hav knit 40 pare of socks fo the solgers and it take all i can earn to get bread . . . if you cud hear the crys of my little children i think you wod fell for us i am pore in this world but i trust rich in heven i trust in god . . . and hope he will Cos you to have compashion on the pore."

A widow whose supporting son was in the army, and whose small farm was about to be sold for a fifty-dollar debt wrote dolefully: "It is with and aking hart and tremelous hand I seat my self this morning to inform you of my condition. . . . [I fear] the Specerlators will prove too hard for us as we have evry thing to by and so little to by with som times I am all most reddy to giv up the strugle as thar is no ey to pitty or hand to swath her[e] I lie in a pore neighborhood those that can assist the nedy will not do so they all have and excuse. . . . I had one side of bacon from the

[45]

Govement the summer after my son left is all I have had I am in my 72 year . . . pleas excuse bad speling and writing and help me if you pleas."

Another woman wrote : "Mr govner Vance Sier I now Seate myself to drop you a few lines to let you [know] mi condition and in witch way the people are treating of me mi husban is bin in Survas over twelve months and I have never received eny thing from the county yet only . . . three dollars for my Self and one dollar and a half for mi youngest child at five years old and I have two more children one nine and the nother eleven . . . I have one nag and Seven hed of hogs and I am nerly out of corn and I have bin walking the laste five dayes and have not got eny yet I had not the money but I barred it and then the[y] refused to take it the[y] Say the[y] are afraid it will bee no count . . . I now Sende this to you fore advice . . . the pore soldiers are in the army wading thru mud and water and fighting fore our bee loved cuntry while nothers at home a specerlating of[f] ove the pore women . . . and now Ses the[y] have got as murch of the Confedret money as the[y] wante and refuses to take it . . . I thinke ther are a wating fore a hier price and du thinke it is harde fore me and mi children while thare is a nuf in the nabourhood hosanna blessed is the king of israel that cometh in the mane [name] of the lord yours truly."

One woman told of her misery in even greater detail: "I sent to Warrenton yestiday and they Said the govnerment had not put any thing there for the Soldiers wifes I never have suferd so much as I have for the last three or four months for I have to go Some times week[s] with nothing but bread to eat and I think that is to hard to take a poor man from his wife and children to leave hear to perish to death when we go to these rich people bout hear they wont let us have not one pound of meal for less than 50 cent . . . we have com mity in our district but they will not do any thing for us . . . if you dont provide some way for us to live we will be compell to take our little children and [go] to our Husband or they must Come home to us."

Another was even more ominous in tone: "Sir we take the privilege of writing you a fiew lines to inform you of a fiew things that is mooving at this time in the state of NC the time has come that we the common people has to hav bread or blood & we are bound booth men & women to hav it or die in the attempt some of us has bin

[47]

travling for the last month with the money in our pockets to buy corn & tryd men that had a plenty & has bin unable to buy a bushel holding on for a better price we are willing to gave & obligate two Dollars a bushel but no more for the idea is that the slave oner has the plantation & the hands to rais the brad stuffs & the common people is drove of[f] in the ware to fight for the big mans negro & he at home making nearly all the corn that is made, & then becaus he has the play in his own fingers he puts the price on his corn so as to take all the Solders wages for a fiew bushels & then . . . [extend credit] until the debt will about take there land & every thing they hav & then they will stop all & if not they will hav to Rent there lands of there lords Sir we hoos sons brothers & husbands is now fighting for the big man's negros are determined to hav bread out of there barns & that at a price that we can pay or we will slaughter as we go . . . we no that this is unlawful at a common time but we are Shut up we cant trade with no body only Just those in the Confedersy . . . & it seems that all harts is turned to gizards. Sir consider this matter over and pleas send us a privat letter of instruction."

That the threats of violence contained in this

and other letters were not mere persiflage is evidenced by bread riots in a number of Southern cities. At Salisbury, North Carolina, a group of women went to some merchants and offered them the prices fixed by the government for military purchases, and when they were refused they broke into the establishments with hatchets and took away a quantity of flour, salt, and molasses. A similar incident was forestalled at Greensboro by nabbing the leaders and putting them in jail. A provision shop in Mobile was raided by a group of hungry women in the spring of 1863; and about the same time a large-scale riot was initiated in Richmond by a group of women marching down the streets, brandishing weapons, and clamoring for bread.

Experiences of humble folk in reference to clothing were very much like those pertaining to food. The similarity was aptly set forth in a poetic taunt of Yankee origin which a Tarheel soldier in 1864 passed on to his home folk:

The ladies down south they do not denigh
They usted to drink the coffey and now they drink
    the rye
They ladies in dixey they are quite in the dark

They used to bye the indigo and now they bile the
Bark.

Not long after the war broke out spinning
wheels and looms were brought from outhouses
and attics and deft hands began the fabrication
of materials to replace the supply of store-bought
clothes. In November, 1861, a North Carolina
woman wrote her soldier husband proudly: "I
do not ask the Yankee any odds if I can get thread
and dye stuffs I can make my own dresses." And
James D. B. De Bow proclaimed in the spring of
1862 that "every household has become a manufacturing establishment; the hum of the spinning-
wheel may be heard in every hamlet and the rattle
of the loom sings the song of better times to our
glorious South."

Many of the poorer women were spinning and
weaving at least a portion of the cloth used in
their households when the war broke out, and
others had desisted from the practice so recently
as to need little refreshing of technique. As a general rule, therefore, the inmates of cabins made
the adjustment to the new clothing order more
readily than did the plantation women. During
the lean days following 1862, many of the poorer

households supplemented their meager incomes by making cloth for their economic superiors. "Some boddy is all wa[y]s after mey and the girls to work for them," wrote a lowly Tarheel mother to her soldier son. "Ben Thorp wife Sent to me to weave a peace of clorth . . . Salla wove 15 teen yards in too days—wove 6 in the day and too in nigh[t] every [one] is push[ed] a weaving the Big folks wants so much work don . . . we is got Soo much work to doo we have to Spin late in night the girls Sas tha wish you was hear to see you[r] new Bed tick."

In some instances women whose husbands were in the army made cloth for neighboring men in return for the plowing of their fields, the cutting of their wood, and the performing of other services. "I got wheat from Rich Harp," wrote one housewife. "I spun flax for him at the old price [and] he let mea have wheat at the old price."

A few women grew indigo for the dye of their homespun clothing, but the majority depended on coloring obtained from walnut hulls, and from the roots, bark, leaves, and berries of sundry vines, trees, and shrubs. Pine roots, for instance, yielded an attractive garnet and the myrtle bush produced a nice gray for woolens. By varying the strength

[51]

of the dye solution, a diversity of shades might be easily obtained. Copperas, produced by soaking pieces of rusty iron in a kettle of water, was used to set or fix the color in thread or cloth. Many women succeeded in making appealing garb of their homespun fabrics.

A Yankee soldier who participated in the Prairie Grove, Arkansas, campaign of December, 1862, noted in his diary that "Three buxom blooming lasses real country beauties dressed with taste and seeming care in striped homespun flannel" were standing in front of their log shanty encouraging the Federals with such expressions as "Go in boys give them h-ll—you are the boys who can whip all the G-d d-md secesh in Arkansas— I'll bet on you fellers."

But the finery displayed by these girls was as unrepresentative of the majority of poor folk as were their disloyal sentiments. The difficulty of obtaining cotton cards—the wire-toothed brushes used in preparing the lint cotton for spinning— was the principal crux in the clothing situation. Southern governors made tremendous efforts to obtain cards by blockade-running and by domestic manufacture, and to make them available to their constituents—particularly to soldiers' families—

at reasonable prices. But the supply was far from adequate to the needs.

In North Carolina, and in other states as well, some relief was afforded by the practice of taking cotton and wool to textile mills for carding and spinning but frequently the owners refused to perform this service except in exchange for grain or meat, and many poor people needed these products worse than they needed clothing. "I have went twice to the U[n]ion factory . . . to get me some thread" wrote a distressed North Carolinian to her governor, "and not one single lbs could I get . . . myself and family are very bare indead for clothes . . . the reason that we cannot get thread is that we have not corn or bacon . . . [to] barter . . . my husband has sent me some money to buy thread with but it will not do."

Shoes were harder to get than other items of clothing. Tanning of cowhides entailed a degree of skill and brawn that few manless households possessed. And those who were able to obtain leather by hook or by crook often found the prices charged by shoemakers prohibitive. Some families resorted to wooden footwear or to cloth shoes with soles of wood. Others went barefooted the year round. But some of these latter felt keenly the social restraints imposed by their deprivation. "Half the ladys in Rutherford County hast to Stay at home from church for the want of a pear off Shoes," wrote an anonymous female to Governor Vance in the summer of 1863; "the[y] Say the[y] never did go to church beare footed sence they weare grone and they will haft to Stay [now] or go beare footed. . . . Thears hides enowgh in this naborhood to Shew the people if we cold get them tand on fare terms."

Scarcity of clothing was of particular significance in winter because of the shortage of fuel. Many country people could not pay the cost of cutting and hauling wood. Poor townspeople, being farther removed from the source of supply, suffered more than rural folk; and even the middle-class element sometimes had to observe the strictest economy. "Wood is so scarce," wrote the daughter of a Lenoir, North Carolina, minister in January, 1864, that "we sit together in ma's room & there . . . is so much confusion that I can get nothing done."

Education naturally suffered as a result of the impingements of war, particularly in the rural sections. Children often were required to forego school in the interest of the family livelihood. Books, slates, and other supplies were expensive and scarce. The dearth of horses and carriages made transportation a difficult problem if not a downright impossibility.

A North Carolina woman who spun and wove long hours for the "big folk," in addition to taking care of her own crops, wrote to her soldier son in August, 1864: "5 goes to scoll every day . . . the girls is most throu thear spelling book got . . . six more leaves to Say Miss Adda is going to put theam to redding this weak if tha get ther Bookes." Several weeks later she wrote with obvious disappointment that the sickness of her husband had forced the removal of the boys from school to help her with the grinding of sorghum cane. "The girls is got a 11 more days to goe to school and thear time will bee out Miss Adda Sas she is sorry the girls is got to S[t]op tha learn soo fast . . . I wish you was hear to learn the girls of night when tha stop school Miss Adda . . . told the girls tha had be[a]t all of the rest of her Scollars."

Soldiers often made inquiry of the progress in school of their children, and there can be no doubt that this solicitude, attributable largely to an increased appreciation of learning derived from army experience, was a boon to education.

Most of the elementary schools seem to have been run on a subscription basis. Tuition was often paid in farm products or in cloth. The majority of schoolteachers were women, preachers, or old men, and few of them were well qualified for the role of instructor. Teacher compensation was miserly. A North Carolina woman in 1863 received $20 per month and board for teaching a school that opened at seven-thirty o'clock in the morning and closed at six in the evening. Sessions were generally shortened to two terms of three months or less—one in summer and the other after harvest. Educational activities were discontinued in many border localities, but in most interior communities schools of some sort continued to function throughout the war.

Textbooks of Confederate imprint came into existence in considerable number. Some of these contained choice bits of propaganda. For instance, Johnson's Elementary Arithmetic set forth these problems: (1) "A Confederate soldier captured 8 Yankees each day for 9 successive days; how many did he capture in all?" (2) "If one Confederate soldier can kill 90 Yankees, how many Yankees can 10 Confederate soldiers kill?" (3) "If one Confederate soldier can whip 7 Yankees, how many soldiers can whip 49 Yankees?" But books used by most Rebel scholars consisted of such favorites of prewar days as Webster's spellers, McGuffey's readers, and Davies' arithmetics.

The hardships produced by war were alleviated occasionally by diversions of various sorts. Members of both sexes assembled for cornhuskings in the fall and early winter. "We had [a] gae corn Shuking," wrote a North Carolina mother to her son in November, 1864. "The croud . . . put all of the Shukes away that night Doc will Shuk his corn next." Women had all-day quilting parties and spinning bees where work was combined pleasantly with gossip. These occasions apparently lost none of their merriment when refreshments were reduced to roasted sweet potatoes, gingerbread, molasses candy, and cereal coffee. The meetings of sewing and knitting societies pledged to the making of clothes for soldiers were usually marked by sprightly conversation. Younger women occasionally inserted slips of paper containing their names and addresses into their finished handiwork; and

[57]

sometimes poetic sentiments calculated to edify and amuse the soldier recipient were included. One girl adorned her card with this combination of profundity and nonsense:

Never Saw I the righteous forgotten

Full many a gem of purest ray serene
The dark unfathomed caves of ocean bear;
Full many a flower is born to blush unseen
And waste its sweetness on the desert air.

P.S. Apples are good but peaches are better
If you love me, you will write me a letter.

In some parts of the South, country people made a social occasion of the cutting of a bee tree. "Lamon . . . is going to cut his Beetree," wrote a young Tarheel to a friend in 1863, "and you no that he will invite every person in this part of the country . . . tell my frind Mr. Lewis to come and bring . . . the Black bottle and we will put up with what will mix with it." Perhaps the practice of taking along the "black bottle" explains in part the enthusiastic comment of another correspondent concerning an affair in a neighboring community: "We found a Bee-tree near Philadelphus —had a number of ladies at the cutting—the tree had neither bees nor honey—the crowd though seemed to enjoy it as much as if there had been ten gallons."

Rural people continued to derive enjoyment in summer from picnics, fishing, and barbecues. Holiday seasons, especially Christmas, were marked by rounds of parties that featured games and dancing. Singing, in small groups and on such a scale as to merit the designation of musical sprees and singing schools, was an important source of diversion throughout the war. Correspondence of the times indicates the popularity of such songs as "Dixie," "Bonnie Blue Flag," "Maryland," "Lorena," "All Quiet Along the Potomac Tonight," "Farewell to Brother Jonathan," "God Save the South," "The Girl I Left Behind Me," "When This Cruel War Is Over," "Gay and Happy Still," and "Wait for the Wagon." But among rural people the folk songs and sentimental favorites of ante-bellum days were generally preferred to tunes which drew their inspiration from the war. "Home Sweet Home" ranked high in the esteem of country singers, along with "Annie Laurie," "Juanita," "Her Bright Eyes Haunt Me Still," "Annie of the Vale," "Sweet Evelena," and "Lilly Dale."

Older men found diversion mainly in informal

get-togethers at county court sessions and at cross-roads stores where conversation—punctuated by meditative puffs at corncob pipes and spitting of tobacco juice—leaned to politics, community trivia, and the vicissitudes of war. Boys amused themselves with such customary juvenile recreations as marbles, mumble-peg, wrestling, jumping, and swimming. Fathers and older brothers in the army occasionally sent home the requisite powder and lead for hunting.

Courting afforded considerable diversion for the young folk, though the scarcity of eligible males created special problems. "I am still flying around with the girls," wrote a teen-age youngster to his bachelor uncle in the army; "I tell you they keep me sterred up. I went to meting . . . at Union and coming home I had to keep company with about a dozen girls and you know that they keep me stirede up. I want you to make haste and kill these old Yankies by Christmas and come home to help me out for I tell you that I have my hands full." Another young beau indicated similar difficulties. "You said you wanted me to keep the girls from going wild," he wrote his soldier cousin. "That [is] hard to do with some of them . . . all they want is aman So you must come hom with

Hugh this fall and I will try to make arun and we will have a fly round with the girls and have a big spree."

Much of the love-making was done at church functions, particularly at summer revivals. A Virginia cavalryman wrote to a friend in Rockingham County: "right to me a bout the big meating and how you in joyed your self and how menny girls you Sqese." And a North Carolinian reporting to a soldier correspondent said: "At Camp meating the boys an girls did not fly round the black stumps much they was a great many wounded soldiers there the girls did not set back much this year like they allways did . . . i recon the reason of that was that the boys did not Suit them."

When unattached soldiers went home on furlough they made the rounds of picnics, singings, and parties; and often they found it impossible to meet all the social demands occasioned by their visits. "I did not marrie whiles I was at home," wrote a young Alabaman in the closing days of the conflict, "but you would have thought I would if [you] had of seen me. . . . The gi[r]les was more friendly than ever I saw them in my life they is getting very tired of this war, they all wants it to end. I do too." In view of the concentrated social activity occasioned by circumstances such as these, it is not surprising that the Confederacy witnessed a series of marriage epidemics.

War has ever been conducive to moral and spiritual deterioration and the Confederacy offered no exception to the general rule. In the early months of the war many preachers joined the army, and later on others were forced by the mounting cost of living to forsake the pulpit for more lucrative employment. Attendance at church services dwindled because of the absence of menfolk and because of the difficulties of travel. "The ways of Zion languish and mourn," observed the Mississippi Synod in 1863. "Pastors are parted from their flocks, God's worship interrupted or forbidden, while from many churches God's people are exiled sheep scattered without their shepherd."

Religious disorganization and apathy was accompanied by an increase of crime and an ebbing of morals. In Richmond and in other cities garroteers, drunkards, and prostitutes roamed the streets with comparative impunity. In rural areas of the interior, conditions were not nearly so bad; but in border sections and in the deserter country, brigandage and vice flourished. A Confederate major stationed in East Tennessee wrote in 1863 to his wife: "I will state as a matter of history that female virtue if it ever existed in this country seems now almost a perfect wreck. Prostitutes are thickly crowded through mountain & valley, in hamlet & city." And a Mississippian remarked that if a dead man were found on the streets of Ellisville in Jones County, authorities would "pay no more attention than if it was a dog." The disruption of the local court system made law enforcement a mockery in many localities.

Despite state legislation forbidding the distillation of spirits from grain and from other food products, an enormous amount of whisky and brandy was manufactured and consumed throughout the Confederacy. "William McLean Died the 3 Day of January by hard drink," wrote a North Carolinian to his son in 1862. "I believe Liquor is doing more harm than the war. Every body is [s]tilling that can get a still." The mountain country was a favorite haven of the whisky makers. A Tarheel wrote Governor Vance in 1864: "Thar is now and has bin for the last Three months Sum Twelve or fifteen stills running night and day . . . most of the men who own the Stills lives in South Carolina and tha have imploid the poorest men tha can find So as to Ignore the Fine . . . if it is

[63]

not Stopt . . . the poor people must and will Starve for the want of bread these abominable law breakers are paing from Thirty to forty Dollars pir bushel for corn." Another North Carolinian wrote to his brother: "There are many church members who have gone into the *whiskey* business . . . many members of churches are drinking and getting drunk constantly."

But it is easy to exaggerate the prevalence of evil-doing. In the face of the widespread degeneration which the war called forth there were large numbers who remained steadfast in character and in religion. Letters of poor people to relatives in the army and to the state governors frequently indicate a religious sincerity and a humble reliance on divine providence.

What of the morale of the poor folk? Indications are that they supported the war in its early stages with no less zeal than their upper-class neighbors. But as the conflict dragged on into the second and third years, there was a notable defection of spirit, particularly among the wives and mothers of soldiers; and by the summer of 1864, if not sooner, the majority of them would probably have welcomed peace on the basis of emancipation of slaves and the restoration of the Union.

Several factors contributed to the disheartening of the poorer classes. Paramount among these was the feeling that privileged groups, particularly the planters, were shirking their military responsibilities. This opinion derived mainly from the law exempting the owner of twenty slaves from military service, and from the failure of planters to meet the requisitions of army leaders for Negroes to work on fortifications. Dissatisfaction on these scores gained currency from the airings of local politicians who bore grievances against the Davis administration. A Mississippian wrote his governor in the fall of 1862 that the twenty-Negro law was "the handle at which most of the malcontents grind." A soldier who wrote to Vance in June, 1863, asking for a furlough to harvest his small crop of grain remarked significantly: "how can we go in to battle and fight to keep the enemy back of[f] the rich man who beca[u]se he owns twenty negros is permitted to stay at home with his family and save his grain but the [poor] man must suffer in the armmy for somthing to eat his family suffering at home for somthing to eat."

Another factor which depressed mightily the spirit of the poor was the conviction that the "big folk" were using the war to enhance their riches.

A Georgian wrote his brother in 1862 that "lyeing, Swindling and a Speculation is all that is goinge on here now thare is but littel sade about war here all that has the means to go on is a trying to Seake and devour evry thing . . . theare is a heap of Yankies here as well as in [the] North." As the war went on there was an increasing protest against slaveowners' hoarding foodstuffs while the families of soldiers were reduced to the verge of starvation. Thousands of impoverished people doubtless were of the opinion expressed by a North Carolina woman who beseeched Governor Vance to detail her husband to home service so that her crying children might be fed. "i would like to know what he is fighting for," she said; "he has nothing to fight for i don't think that he is fighting for anything only for his family to starve."

Distress caused by suffering of loved ones in the army was another depressing influence. A North Carolinian wrote to his brother in 1863, urging him to desert. "I would advise you to . . . go to the other side," he said, "whear you can get plenty and not stay in this one horse barefooted naked and famine stricken Southern Confederacy."

Reverses suffered by the South on the field of battle had a decidedly disheartening effect on the poorer folk. The defeats at Gettysburg and Vicksburg followed by Bragg's failure at Chattanooga were depressing enough, but the fall of Atlanta and Hood's defeat in Tennessee utterly destroyed the hope of many people. In January, 1865, one of Governor Vance's correspondents who signed her letter, "A Poor Woman and Children," remarked: "You know as well as you have a head that it is impossible to whip they Yankees, there for I beg you for God sake to try and make peace on some terms . . . why sir every state has been over run but North Carolina and now you see that they Yankees are doing as they pleas in South Carolina, we haven got the forses . . . I believe slavery is doomed to dy out that god is agoing to liberate niggers and fighting anylonger is fighting *against* God." A short time later Lee wrote Vance that an increasing tide of desertion was being provoked by letters of despair flooding the camps of his army. Efforts were made to renew the spirits of the people, but these were of little avail.

A final and significant factor tending to undermine morale was the crushing weight of hardship which fell upon the poorer women of the Confederacy. Their long hours of labor at plows and spinning wheels constituted the lesser part of their woes. Far more distressing was the mental harassment which tormented them—the fear of being unable to provide adequate food and clothing for their children; the dread of disease; anxiety for the safety and welfare of husbands, sons, and other loved ones in the army; the fear of visitation by enemy raiders, or by native marauders; the apprehension of Negro uprisings; and the worry over such innumerable trials of farm operation as the breaking down of equipment, the deterioration of fences, the straying of livestock, and the caprices of the weather. These vexations combined with the obsessing loneliness for absent male companions to break down even the staunchest of spirits. One North Carolina woman who manifested the most stubborn courage against all sorts of difficulties for three and a half years of the conflict was finally moved to write to her soldier son in January, 1865: "Tell theam all to s[t]op fiting and come home to live if you all wod put down you gouns and come home and let the Big men stae the fiting wod Soon Stop if you all Stae theaire you all will bee kild I want you all to come home."

Undoubtedly the greater burden of war was borne not by the ragged followers of Lee and Johnston, but by the poor wives and mothers at home who strove valiantly to provide a livelihood for their dependents. It is remarkable that they bore up under their trials as well as they did. And those humble women who did remain steadfast in labor and loyalty to the end—and their number was considerable—were indeed the greatest heroes of the Lost Cause.

Two of the greatest mistakes of the Confederate government were the refusal to exempt from conscription nonslaveholding adult males upon whose labor the livelihood of wives and small children was vitally dependent, and the failure to take effective measures against hoarding and speculation. Dissatisfaction arising from these sins of omission did more than anything else to break down the morale of the civilian masses. Long before the finale at Appomattox, the doom of the Confederacy had been firmly sealed by the widespread defection of her humblest subjects.

III

THE COLORED FOLK

WHEN the booming guns at Charleston inaug-
urated hostilities between the North and the South
in 1861, there were about three and a half million
slaves living in the eleven states which were to con-
stitute the Confederacy. The effects of war upon
the life of these blacks varied considerably with
time and locale. Day-by-day activities of those in-
habiting interior portions of the South were not
greatly disturbed during the first year of conflict;
and many of those residing in areas untouched
by Federal troops experienced surprisingly little
change from beginning to end of the war.

But in the invaded sections of the Confederacy,
the effects of the coming of the Yankees were immediate and tremendous; and the results were virtually the same whether the invasion was of Virginia in 1861, of Tennessee in 1862, of Mississippi

in 1863, of Georgia in 1864, or of South Carolina in 1865.

One of the first consequences of the approach of Federal troops to a given locality was the exodus of Negroes from that area to the Yankee lines. There can be no definite estimate as to how many or what per cent of slaves ran away to the Federals during the war, but it can be said without fear of exaggeration that the approach of Northern troops to any community initiated a trek of Negroes toward the Yankee camps; and that in many instances the stampede became so great as to carry away the major portion of the black population.

The tendency of the blacks to flock to the Union camps on the approach of the invaders is well illustrated by the case of Shirley Plantation in Virginia. The Federals came first to this vicinity on June 30, 1862. There is no evidence in the records of any slaves having run off before this time. But on July 14, two weeks after the arrival of the Union force, the plantation journal records that "15 negro men and boys ran off." A few days later a Negro woman and two children disappeared. Shortly afterwards the Federals withdrew. On July 13, 1863, the Yankees made their second appearance in the vicinity. Within the next three days, fifteen Negro men took flight to "Yankeedom." On April 5, 1864; the Federals again came to the environs of Shirley, this time in greater force than previously. After a month of quiet, during which the slaves were evidently making secret preparations for departure, a grand exodus began. Within four days thirty slaves went to the Yankees. By June 20, seventeen more had left the plantation. This brought the total of fugitives for the three Federal incursions to eighty, a figure which comprehended nearly all of the slaves of this plantation.

The proportion of slaves running away from Shirley may have been exceptional. But an abundance of evidence indicated a close parallel of tendencies in other invaded sections. In August, 1862, a Confederate general estimated that every week a million dollars worth of North Carolina Negroes were fleeing to the Yankees. A Union official wrote from Mississippi that after Pemberton's surrender, "Vicksburg was looked upon by the Negroes as the very gate of heaven, and they came trooping to it as pigeons to their roost at night."

One of the most interesting, and perhaps significant, commentaries on the propensity of the slaves for seeking the Yankee camps when opportunity presented itself is that of a small Virginia girl as

recorded by her mother in a diary. On April 20,
1862, the diarist, who was at that time residing in
Fredericksburg, noted that the full band of the
Federal army encamped across the river was playing "Yankee Doodle" and the "Star Spangled
Banner." Entries in the diary after that date indicate that Negroes were stealing away across the
river in ever-increasing numbers. Naturally the departure of the slaves became a common topic of
conversation in Fredericksburg. One day in early
August, 1862, the diarist's little daughter, Nannie
Belle, and Sallie, a neighbor's child, were playing
"ladies." Sallie, pretending to be a woman making
a neighborly call, said to Nannie Belle, "Good
morning, ma'm, how are you today?" Whereupon
Nannie Belle replied with a sigh: "I don't feel very
well this morning. All of my niggers have run away
and left me."

Drastic steps were taken by state and Confederate authorities to prevent the escape of Negroes
to the Federals. Picket lines were doubled in some
sections; the passport system was rigidly applied
in others. Local organizations were formed
throughout invaded areas under such designations
as "home guards," "independent scouts," and
"mounted pickets" to assist in keeping the slaves

with their owners. Threats of severe punishment for attempts to escape were made by masters. The churches cast their influence on the side of the harassed planters by expelling from membership Negroes who sought the Federal camps. The record book of a Virginia Baptist congregation contains this entry for September 17, 1864: "Martha . . . was excluded from the fellowship of the church for fornication . . . church lists revised. Forty-one excluded who have gone off to the enemy." But the lure of freedom and the ingenuity of the blacks in contriving means of escape were usually great enough to overcome all these obstacles.

Another noticeable effect of Federal invasion was the tendency among Negroes in areas near the Union lines to become insubordinate and insolent toward owners and overseers. A typical case is that of a Virginia coachman who, after the Federals told him that he was free, went immediately to his master's closet, helped himself to a splendid suit of clothes, a watch and chain, and a walking stick. After adorning himself with this finery the servant returned to the parlor and told his master that in future he must drive his own coach.

Several years ago an intelligent ex-slave of Pulaski, Tennessee, told the writer that Negroes of his county celebrated the approach of the Yankees with songs containing impudent thrusts at the whites, as:

De ladies in Tennessee wuz a gittin' mighty
    gran'—
Hoop-skirts and petticoats a draggin' on de
    groun',
Bonnets on dey shoulders and dey noses to de sky—
Bye and Bye will come a time, big pig, or little pig,
Root hog or die;
Old Tennessee used to drink coffee but now she
    drinks rye.

.   .   .   .

Oh black gal, you can't shine,
I done quit foolin' wid de kinky-headed kin';
First of July and de las' of May,
I've had a white gal on my min'.

.   .   .   .

Ole massa come down de road dis mornin',
Wif de muffstash on he face;
He grab he hat and he lef' very sudden,
Lak he gwine to leave de place;
Ole massa runned away,
And de darkey stayed at home;

It must now be very confiscatin';
De Lincum soldiers come;
Dere's wine and cider in de cellar,
And de niggers must hab some.

The exasperation of the whites when subjected to Negro insolence in invaded areas is illustrated by an incident that took place in Helena, Arkansas, early in 1865. Two white men, Powell and Yates, walking down the street were greeted by a Negro. Powell returned the salutation with the greeting, "Howdy, Uncle." The Negro replied with an oath that he did not permit such people as Powell to claim kin with him. "Call me mister," the Negro added angrily. When the two whites had walked on out of the Negro's hearing, Powell said to Yates, "Oh my God; how long before my ——— will be kicked by every Negro that meets me."

The insubordination of slaves frequently took the form of refusing to continue work after the approach of the Federals. The correspondence of Mrs. C. C. Clay, of Northern Alabama with her son, Senator Clement C. Clay, is replete with complaints of Negro idleness. In February, 1863, she wrote that "one piece of cloth had been woven in the time I used to have ten. . . . We cannot make

[76]

any cotton unless a speedy change takes place."
The next month she bemoaned: "The slaves are
ignorant and grasping. . . . I have a hard time
with ours for they just do as they list. I try by
'moral suasion' to get them to do their duty—and
it sometimes succeeds." Still later she wrote:
"They say they *are* free. We cannot exert any authority. I beg ours to do what little is done. Lu-
cinda makes the beds. Maria gets the morsel we eat
for we have just sufficient to keep us from starvation. She and Critty milk two cows but grumble and
threaten."

But the Clay slaves were less slothful than some
in other invaded areas. At Magnolia in Louisiana
the Negroes were so completely demoralized by
the coming of the Federals in 1862 that the overseer was finally provoked to write in the plantation
journal: "I wish every negro would leave the place
as they will do only what pleases them, go out in
the morning when it suits them, come in when they
please, etc." Slaves in all invaded areas began to
demand wages for their work shortly after the arrival of the Yankees. In some cases the planters
were able to postpone the adoption of the wage
system by promises, presents, and other induce-
ments. But eventually the importunities of the

workers forced a general acquiescence in some plan of cash compensation.

Refusal to submit to punishment was another form of insubordination common among slaves throughout invaded portions of the South. A senile Texan attempted to whip a recalcitrant Negro in the summer of 1863. The servant resisted and, according to the report of a neighbor, "cursed the old man all to pieces," walked off in the wood, and then sent back word that he would not return unless a pledge of impunity were given him. His terms were accepted and he came back.

Planters in this and in other communities actually became afraid to punish their slaves. A Tennessee woman wrote to her soldier husband in 1863 that "overseers generally are doing very little good, and they complain of the negroes getting so free and idle, but I think it is because most everyone is afraid to correct them. I tried to correct one negro for a thing last summer; it would frighten Mr. Ashford [the overseer] out of his wits almost." Three Alabama slaves threatened to kill the overseer on the C. C. Clay plantation, if he attempted to punish them. Mrs. Clay went so far as to go to a colored woman who had threatened to burn a dwelling if she were punished, and to beg the slave to think of the "sin" of her proposed action.

In many instances Federal invasion caused outbursts of violence among the slaves. Frequently these uprisings took the form of seizure and destruction of the master's property and riotous celebration of the advent of freedom. Slaves on the plantation of Governor Thomas O. Moore of Louisiana "had a perfect jubilee" for the "space of a week," according to a neighbor's report to the governor, when Yankee raiders appeared in the vicinity. "Every morning," wrote the neighbor to Moore, "I could see the beeves being driven up from the woods to the quarters—and the number they killed of them it is impossible to tell." The furniture was taken from the owner's house and distributed among the Negro shacks.

When the Federals passed on, most of the adult Negroes followed them, taking as much of the master's property as they could transport and regretfully leaving that which they could not carry. Little wonder is it that the correspondent reporting the affair to the governor ejaculated: "Confound them, they deserve to be half-starved and to be worked nearly to death for the way they acted. . . . They are the greatest hypocrits and liars that God ever made."

The overseer of Magnolia Plantation reported that the approach of the Federals incited the slaves to unrestrained festivity. On one plantation, he said, the Negroes "Rose and Destroyed everything they could get hold of. . . . Pictures, Portraits, and Furniture were all smashed up." Some of the blacks marched around over the countryside "with flags and drums shouting 'Abe Lincoln and Freedom.' "

There were similar disturbances when the Federals invaded South Carolina. At Pooshee Plantation the slaves "cleaned out the storeroom and the meat room." At Whitehall, after being told by the Union troops to help themselves, the Negroes "rushed into the house and took beds, carpets and everything."

The numerous slaves of R. F. W. Allston of South Carolina seem to have reverted to a state of savagery when the Federals arrived. On one Allston plantation, the blacks locked the overseer in the house, and placed an armed Negro at the door with instructions to shoot him if he attempted to escape or to interfere with their plundering. From another Allston plantation the harassed overseer wrote: "I have been Compeld . . . to give up the Barn Key. . . . I would have moved away but have no means to do so . . . on Sunday . . . two Yankeys came up and turned the people loose to distribet the house which they did taking out everything and then to the smoke house and Store Room doing the same . . . the hogs in the Pen is Kild, . . . the Pore mules has been Road to death all most—after this the People have puld down the mantle Pieces, taken off all the doors and windows Cut the banisters and sawed out all such as they wanted."

When report of these disorders came to Mrs. Allston, she and her daughter went to Guendalos Plantation to investigate. No sooner had they arrived than they were surrounded by a crowd of howling, threatening "freedom-intoxicated" slaves. As they danced about their mistress and her daughter brandishing rice hoes, pitchforks, guns, and hickory sticks, they chanted weird verses the words of which were incomprehensible to the whites, followed by a much repeated chorus:

> I free, I free,
> I free as a frog,

I free till I fool,
Glory Alleluia.

Only the composure of the white women kept them from suffering bodily injury.

In a considerable number of cases the approach of the Federals incited the Negroes to acts of personal violence against the whites. Two slaves "mercilessly whipped" an old woman near Canton, Mississippi, in 1863. A patrolman who returned a fugitive in Louisiana in 1862 was mortally wounded from ambush just after he delivered the slave to his master. Negroes on the David Pugh Plantation attacked the owner and his overseer and injured them severely. A Natchez resident traveling in Louisiana in 1863 was attacked, robbed, and then brutally murdered by Negroes. In several instances slaves fired on Confederate pickets. Two refugee Virginia planters who returned to their homes after the passing of a Federal raid were seized by their slaves, subjected to great abuse, and then murdered with shotguns. Criminal attacks of blacks upon white women were rare, but there is certainly a sufficiency of evidence on this point to blast the postwar statement of a Southern planter that "no woman in the whole South was ever molested by a negro during the Civil War."

It would be erroneous to leave the impression that disorder and insubordination were universal among slaves of invaded areas; for there were some who manifested a high degree of loyalty and affection in the midst of the most trying circumstances. Many pieces of silver in use by Southerners today were concealed from the Yankees by faithful domestics. In several instances Negroes upbraided the Federals for mistreating their "white folks." During the long nights of uncertainty and fear incident to invasion, black guardians kept watch over white women and children and reassured them with repeated promises to sacrifice life itself for their protection. But instances of such positive loyalty were exceptional, and restricted largely to the house servants who, because of their privileged status, had perhaps more to lose than to win by freedom.

Sometimes even trusted domestics abandoned their masters during the stress of invasion and went in quest of the uncertainties of freedom. "Those we loved best, and who loved us best—as we thought—were the first to leave us," wrote a Virginian; and other owners told sorrowfully of house servants turning over keys to Yankee plunderers.

All in all, the reaction of slaves to the coming of the Federals was such as to reveal to the whites how little they knew of the real feelings so effectively concealed behind the veil of smiles and obsequious manners. And people who boast today that they "know the nigger" might well learn a lesson from the experience of their Confederate progenitors. Before the war was over most whites living in areas penetrated by Federal troops had abundant reason to feel as did an Alabaman who in 1863 complained that the " 'faithful slave' is about played out."

In considering the demoralization that prevailed throughout invaded sections it is important to bear in mind the fact that only a minority of the total slave population lived in regions penetrated by the Yankees. For the effects of war upon the majority it is necessary to focus attention upon the vast areas that lay beyond the reach of the men in blue.

The conduct of slaves in these areas was much more orderly than in regions that felt the direct influence of invasion. But the comparative quietude of these slaves should not be interpreted as a willing acquiescence in bondage or an indifference to the outcome of the war. Many Negroes of the interior South were of the opinion that freedom was an issue of the conflict even in its early stages, and after Lincoln's Proclamation, ignorance of the connection between Union victory and emancipation seems to have been exceptional. Most of the slaves earnestly desired freedom, and when it came within safe and convenient reach they seized upon it with alacrity. Some went into wild effusions of joy. A Virginia Negro when informed of his liberation ran out to the barnyard and jumped from one strawstack to another, screaming at the highest pitch of his voice. And a colored woman waked the folk at the big house late at night with cries of "Thank Gawd! Thank Gawd! Thank Gawd A'Mighty!"

Both Northerners and Southerners of Civil War times were somewhat surprised at the failure of the slaves to attempt large-scale insurrections. But to present-day students this circumstance holds no mystery. The only Negroes qualified to lead such undertakings were, with a few exceptions, house servants, and this group was closely bound to the whites by ties of association and affection; communication over large areas was virtually impossible; and the great majority of slaves were of a nonviolent, opportunistic disposition. They deemed it better, therefore, to wait for deliverance by the Yankees than to resort prematurely to bloody attacks upon their powerful overlords.

The prevailing attitude was aptly summed up by an alleged conversation between two Negroes early in the war. One of them, speculating on the effects of the conflict, suggested that the slaves might eventually take up arms for their deliverance.

"Yo talkin' fool talk, nigger," the other rejoined; "ain' you neber been see two dogs fightin' ober bone 'fo now?"

"Cose I is—but I dunno what dat dar got to do wid dis here."

"Well," came the retort, "yo aint neber been see de bone fight none, is yo?"

While the Negroes of the interior regions waited for freedom the war necessitated some adjustments in their manner of life. One of the most significant of these had to do with labor. In times of peace the bulk of farm work had been devoted to the production of cotton. But the blockade of Southern ports, Federal occupation of the meat and grain districts of Kentucky and Tennessee, and the necessity of sustaining a large army led to a widespread movement after 1861 to replace cotton with food crops.

At first de-emphasis of cotton was attempted by voluntary pledges, but tardiness of some planters in complying with the restrictive program caused a resort to legislative prohibitions. By the spring of 1863, most states had passed laws compelling the reduction of cotton to an amount not exceeding three acres per hand. The combined effects of public sentiment and of legislation appear to have limited cotton acreage in 1863 and 1864 to about one fourth or one fifth of the prewar average.

As cotton production was curtailed, the labor of slaves thus released was turned to the growth of foodstuffs. Fields of the Alabama Black Belt that in the 1850's were flecked with white as far as the eye could see now presented mosaics of sorghum cane, potato vines, and corn. Throughout the length and breadth of the Confederacy "King Cotton" yielded the majority of his domain to such vital products as cowpeas, sweet potatoes, soy beans, peanuts, oats, barley, and wheat.

Available testimony indicates that Negro workers adapted themselves to the program of diversification with marked success. The food grown in the uninvaded portions of the Confederacy was ample for the needs of the entire Southern population, both civilian and military. And while it cannot be denied that hunger bedeviled both the army and a portion of the home folk, this was due not to inadequacies of production, but rather to failure of distribution.

Crops would have been even more bountiful if the war had not disrupted labor supervision. At first many overseers and owners were permitted to remain at home under exempting clauses of the conscription acts. But unpopularity of this policy among nonslaveholders, plus increasing demands for soldiers, led after 1863 to induction into military service of the majority of accustomed farm directors. Their supervisory functions were taken over largely by women, boys, and old men. In many instances the immediate oversight of plantations was entrusted to responsible Negroes who in peacetime had acted as drivers or foremen.

This modified system of supervision worked well on some plantations, but in the great majority of cases it proved unsatisfactory. Letters of women to state governors and to soldier husbands are replete with complaints concerning the slaves —of their dilly-dallying, of their neglect of fences and plows, and of their mistreatment of livestock. A harassed Texas woman wrote her husband in 1864: "With the prospect of another 4 years war you may give your negroes away . . . and I'll move into a white settlement and work with my hands. . . . The Negroes care no more for me than if I was an old free darkey and I get so mad sometimes that I think I dont care . . . if Myers beats the last one of them to death. I cant stay with them another year alone."

Many other feminine supervisors had less difficulty, but the conclusion is inescapable in the light of the best evidence that the work of slaves deteriorated greatly when deprived by the war of the accustomed management.

Another notable incident of the war was the diversion of workers from fields to factories and mines. In 1861 and 1862 old manufacturing establishments were expanded and new ones set up for the making of guns, ammunition, wagons, uniforms, shoes, saddles, bridles, soap, salt, candles, and numerous other products for soldiers and civilians. Some of these enterprises employed Negroes from the beginning, and the great majority had to depend on colored workmen to an increasing extent as whites were called into the ranks. The blacks were used principally for the heavier work, but enough of them were employed at skilled tasks to weaken considerably the argument of conservative agrarians that colored labor could not be adapted to an industrial economy.

The war had less effect upon the food of slaves than upon their labor. In invaded areas there were recurrent periods when the fare was scant, but in most other sections Negroes had an abundance of edibles throughout the period of conflict. There was some change, however, in the items of diet. The difficulty of obtaining salt led in some instances to a reduction of the meat ration. But planters usually compensated for this deficiency by issuing liberal allowances of molasses. Sweet potatoes were also enjoyed in greater abundance during the war than before. It is not at all unlikely that the shift of emphasis from cotton to food crops resulted in a general improvement of the slave diet during the Confederate period.

Clothing of slaves was modified considerably as a result of the Federal blockade. Homespun garments had generally given way to factory-made suits in the forties and fifties, but during the war there was a reversion by most planters to the practice of spinning, weaving, and making up the clothes of both Negroes and whites at home.

Wool was grown much more extensively during the war than before, but the supply was never equal to the demand. Cotton was usually available in abundance, but the difficulty of procuring the steel-toothed cards for combing the yarn prior to spinning often led to a scarcity of the lighter materials needed for summer suits. Some planters were reduced to the expedient of cutting up carpets and curtains in order to meet the clothing need of their servants. But such drastic measures were rarely necessary before the last winter of the war.

Hats were made of cloth scraps and of palmetto. Buttons were fashioned from small pieces of wood or from persimmon seeds. Shoes presented the greatest difficulty of all clothing items. Tanneries were set up on most plantations, and slave craftsmen achieved fair success as cobblers. But the supply of leather, particularly of the heavy type required for soles, was never adequate. Some planters sought to remedy the deficiency by attaching uppers of cloth or leather to wooden soles. A few resorted to shoes made entirely of wood. But this resulted in protests from plantation mistresses on the score of noise. And some improvident slaves infuriated their masters by using the wooden footgear for kindling.

The few privileges and pleasures enjoyed by slaves in days of peace consisted mainly of visiting neighboring quarters on Sundays, having respite from work on Saturday afternoons, hunting rabbits, opossums, and other small game, attending church services, raising a few pigs, chickens, or turkeys—for home use or for sale—going to barbecues or picnics at laying-by time, attending weddings, and dancing occasionally in the cotton shed or the sugarhouse.

These simple diversions suffered considerable curtailment during the early days of the war, for the increased fear of slave uprisings that accompanied Federal attack caused a general tightening of control agencies.

Long after hostilities had ended, writers and speakers were wont to descant upon the perfect confidence that masters reposed in their slaves during the dark days of conflict, but these testimonials do not square with repressive measures enacted at the time. During the first years of the Confederacy every state passed laws requiring that patrols give more frequent and more serious attention to surveillance of Negro activities, and slave codes were revised so as to lessen the likelihood of conspiracy and rebellion. Use by Negroes of boats and other means of transportation was restricted; penalties for furnishing slaves with firearms and with liquor were increased; and the practice of blacks' living on plantations without white supervision was prohibited.

Repressive state legislation was matched by similar action on the part of municipalities. Individual owners for a time lived up to prewar regulations requiring that slaves not be allowed to go beyond the limits of the plantation without a pass, and that they not be permitted to assemble in groups of over five or six without white escort. But as weeks passed into months and months into years without uprisings actually breaking out, owners and officials tended to relapse into unconcern as to the doings of their servants. Vigilance and attempts at restriction may have been revived by such disturbing phenomena as the Emancipation Proclamation, but the induction of a large proportion of able-bodied white men into military service made enforcement of regulations difficult. On the whole, slaves seem to have enjoyed as much, if not more, freedom during the war than before.

Scarcity of arms and ammunition probably curtailed hunting of such game as squirrels, coons, and rabbits, but quest for the lowly opossum was not affected by these deficiences. Throughout the deep South fishing, picnicking, and visiting flourished during the greater part of the conflict. Scarcity of white ministers and deterioration of wardrobes diminished somewhat the splendor of weddings and funerals, but other religious activities were less disturbed by these contingencies.

The conviction that religious services were a stimulant to submissiveness and industry caused masters and churchmen to exert themselves mightily to keep the spiritual program going. And from numerous pulpits white divines—or if these were not procurable, trusted black exhorters—regaled colored congregations with such texts as "Servants obey your masters," "Let every man wherein he is called abide therein with God," and "Render unto Caesar the things that are Caesar's and unto God the things that are God's." Such themes as "Ye shall know the truth and the truth shall make you free" and the deliverance of the children of Israel from Egyptian bondage were of course studiously avoided.

In meetings attended by whites—as many of them were—a correct attitude was consistently manifested by the slaves. Blessings were often asked by black leaders on the Southern cause, and sometimes defeat was besought for the Yankees. But now and then the colored folk were able to assemble secretly in their own places of worship; there they let go with sincere prayers for Federal victory and "the day of jubilo," and gave themselves to ecstatic singing of such songs as "No Man Can Hinder Me," and "Way Over in the Promised Land."

There was a considerable group of people in the Confederacy who thought that the rights and privileges of slaves should be increased in some particulars, and to this end they launched a movement to humanize the "peculiar institution." The reformers, led by James A. Lyon of Mississippi and Calvin H. Wiley of North Carolina, consisted largely of churchmen. Their program contained several proposals, including: first, repeal of the laws that forbade the teaching of slaves to read, so that Negroes might have the benefit of a direct perusal of the Scriptures; second, abolition of absentee ownership of slaves; third, limited acceptance of testimony of slaves in murder cases, so that overseers or owners could not take the lives of Negroes with impunity simply because of the absence of white witnesses; fourth, legal recognition of slave marriages; and fifth, passage of laws preventing the selling of children away from their parents.

These proposals were discussed widely by religious groups, and they won some support among laymen as well as ministers. Lyon succeeded in getting a bill entitled "An act regulating the marriage and parental relations existing between slaves" introduced in the Mississippi Legislature early in 1865, but the committee to which it was referred thought the time inopportune for its consideration. The reaction of the country at large was very similar to that of this legislative committee, the overwhelming sentiment being that rectification of the "peculiar institution" should not be attempted until the war was won. But there can be no doubt that the establishment of Southern independence would have witnessed the development of a strong movement to purge slavery of its most flagrant evils. And it is possible that this humanitarian impulse which dated back to the days of Thomas Jefferson, but which had been driven under cover by the abolitionist onslaught, would have led eventually to the abolition of slavery itself.

The evil with which reformers found greatest fault—that of breaking up families—derived mainly from the slave trade. It might logically have been expected that the war would cause a marked decline in the buying and selling of Negroes. But this was not the case. Newspaper reports indicate a heavy volume of trade during the first two years of conflict. Confidence in Confederate success was strong, and slaves were regarded by many as good investments. The removal of planters from invaded sections to temporary homes in the interior caused an exceedingly large number of slaves to be offered for sale. Prices in Confederate currency remained high, but there was a decline in values as represented in gold.

The reverses at Gettysburg and Vicksburg caused a slowing down of the slave trade, but in 1864 when Grant failed to take Richmond there was a revival of both confidence and traffic. Sherman's march through Georgia and Hood's defeat in Tennessee reduced buying and selling to a low level, but there was some trading up until the very end of the war. In fact, a few sales were reported after Lee's surrender.

During the last days of the Confederacy the tide of inflation carried slave prices to dizzy heights. John B. Jones recorded in his diary on March 22, 1865, that Negro men were selling in Richmond for $10,000 in Rebel currency. But, of course, the gold equivalent of this fabulous sum was only about $100.

The slaves who experienced the least of freedom and the most of hardship during the war were the ones who labored in military occupations. Hundreds of blacks were engaged as cooks, teamsters, hospital attendants, and railroad repairmen; and the number employed in the construction of defense works ran far into the thousands. The first Confederate volunteers were inclined to balk at menial tasks as unbecoming to their exalted roles as fighters; so Negroes were called upon by military leaders to perform the lowly duties. The exigencies of war considerably modified soldier attitudes toward hard work, but heavy battle casualties required increased use of black labor by the military so as to release every available white man for service in the ranks.

Military work by Negroes consisted mainly of throwing up foundations for heavy artillery, planting obstructions in rivers, building forts, and digging entrenchments. Much of the labor had to be done in marshy country and in extreme weather. Rations were frequently short, and clothing inadequate. Sickness was common, and hospital facilities were deficient. The tendency of workers to run away caused superintendents to frown upon visits to neighboring Negro communities, and the necessity of rushing projects to completion usually prevented the granting of accustomed Saturday afternoon holidays. It is not surprising, then, that Negroes thoroughly detested military labor, and that government agents charged with the impressment of workers became veritable bugaboos in the slave quarter.

Another group of slaves having a military connection enjoyed unusual privileges. These were the body servants who accompanied their masters to camp in the capacity of orderlies. The duties of these colored aides were light, consisting mainly of cooking, laundering, cleaning quarters, shining shoes, and in the cases of those who served cavalrymen, of looking after their masters' horses. A genuine affection, deriving from intimate association that sometimes dated back to early childhood, usually existed between soldiers and their servants. This fact, coupled with the impossibility of exercising a close supervision in the hurly-burly of campaigning, caused masters to give a comparatively free rein to the blacks who shared with them the ups and downs of army life.

Body servants got together frequently for crap shooting and cards. They had abundant opportunity to earn money by washing clothes and performing other services for soldiers who were not so fortunate as to have aides. They were frequently able to supplement army rations by foraging expeditions through the countryside; and their dramatic pleas, which were almost invariably for poor wounded masters, elicited substantial returns even from impoverished citizens.

The servants profited also from victories over the Yankees. After almost any fight sable retainers might be seen walking from the battlefield laden with knives, razors, caps, overcoats, canteens, bacon, and other plunder left by the Federals. The master was given first choice of the spoils, and the remnant was left to the servant's own disposition. Confederate successes such as those of Manassas and Chancellorsville were followed by flush times among black Rebels as well as among white ones.

In view of the close association between soldiers and body servants, it is not surprising that the latter became thoroughly imbued with war ardor. So much so, indeed, that in a number of instances the blacks picked up guns during the pitch of battle and indulged themselves in a few pot shots at the Yankees. Several servants boasted of taking Federal prisoners.

But their greatest contribution was not the wielding of guns. Rather it was the jollity and amusement which they dispensed around the campfire. Their singing, playing, and dancing were effective foes of gloom and nostalgia, and their unfailing cheerfulness gave a powerful fillip to army morale.

There were many Southerners who thought that slaves would make effective soldiers, and they urged the enrollment of large numbers in the army. The most influential of the pioneer advocates of this policy was General Patrick Cleburne. In January, 1864, he presented a paper on the subject to a group of fellow officers in the Army of Tennessee. The preponderance of sentiment at this meeting was unfavorable to Cleburne's scheme, but his paper was forwarded to Richmond. President Davis, fearing the effects of publicizing such a controversial proposal, ordered its suppression.

The desperate need for soldiers, caused by sickness, desertion, and battle casualties, eventually led the government to change its attitude. In December, 1864, Secretary Judah P. Benjamin wrote to a prominent South Carolinian urging him to agitate the arming of the blacks. A few weeks later Davis came out in favor of slave enlistment; about the same time General Lee gave the proposal his endorsement.

On March 13, 1865, the Confederate Congress passed a law authorizing the recruiting of 300,000 Negroes. Most advocates of arming the slaves had argued the necessity of promising freedom to those who should render faithful service, but the law was silent on the subject of emancipation. A few companies of ebon soldiers were organized in Richmond, but as they paraded near the capitol in their spic uniforms they were pelted with mud by contemptuous white urchins who lined the streets. The war ended before colored enlistees had an opportunity to go into battle. But it seems incredible that the ironic experiment of slaves fighting to perpetuate their own bondage could have succeeded.

Negroes were taken into the Northern army to the number of some 200,000. But these soldiers served as freemen, rather than as slaves. Even so, they suffered much discrimination. In several instances white companies refused to serve with them—and once, at least, Negro troops were fired upon by white comrades. The Northern government refused, until the last year of the war, to give colored soldiers equal pay with the whites.

And throughout the conflict Negro troops had to do a disproportionate amount of guarding, policing, ditch digging, and other less pleasant duties of soldiering. When they were given a fair trial on the battlefield they acquitted themselves as creditably as unbiased observers might have expected. Some of them ran when the battle waxed warm, but for such conduct they had ample precedent among their Caucasian associates. Others marched unflinchingly through showers of lead to cross bayonets with yelling Rebels who pounced with demoniacal glee upon their black opponents. When consideration is taken of their background—particularly of the fact that they recently were slaves —it is surprising to find that these black soldiers fought as well as they did.

When the "day of jubilo" finally came it was disappointing to colored civilians as well as to soldiers. The Yankee deliverers showed an unwillingness not only to give the Negroes forty acres and a mule, but even to treat them as freemen. The government herded them into concentration camps where they fell easy prey to exposure and disease; or else they were hired out to adventurers who came South in the wake of Federal invasion to make quick fortunes raising cotton on confiscated plantations. Their new employers often defrauded them of their scanty earnings, subjected them to brutal punishments, and treated them shamefully in respect to food and clothing. True, there were many government officials and private citizens who tried sincerely to deal squarely with them, but these efforts were often thwarted by ignorance and excessive sentimentality.

The early days of freedom were indeed trying ones for blacks and whites alike, and the swell of hatred engendered by war remains today a stumbling block in Southern race relations. Persons of both colors who have the welfare of their respective peoples at heart cannot refrain from wondering now and then whether a better way might not have been found of bringing slavery to an end, if only immoderates in North and South could have been restrained. Peaceful methods would have required a longer time, but they might have achieved an emancipation much more real than that which was vouchsafed at the mouths of cannon.